a bloke for
all seasons

a bloke for all seasons

the **Peter Yealands** story

—— Tom Percy ——

WILY PUBLICATIONS

Published by
Wily Publications Ltd
302 Lake Terrace Road
Shirley
Christchurch 8061
New Zealand
Email: jjhaworth@xtra.co.nz
www.wily.co.nz

ISBN 978-1-927167-02-1

Front cover photo and rear landscape photo of Yealands
Estate Winery by Jim Tannock, Marlborough.

Cover and page design by Quentin Wilson, Christchurch
wilson.quentin@gmail.com

Printed by Taieri Print, Dunedin

CONTENTS

Acknowledgements

My sincere thanks to the many people who have made this book possible: to Martyn Lewis and Vanessa Watson, they will know why; to publisher Jenny Haworth and the team at Wily Publications; to Antoinette Wilson, for all her great work and good advice. Many thanks to the family, friends and colleagues of Peter Yealands for their candid and generous contributions.

Of special note is the unfailing support and encouragement from my wife Annie; without her this could not have been possible. And also of special note: thank you, Peter Yealands, for having such in interesting life.

PROLOGUE

"Maverick" – definition: a person of independent or unorthodox views

It is November 2008 and Peter Yealands has been invited to be a speaker at Thrive Wellington, a national business forum featuring many of New Zealand's captains of industry, eminent entrepreneurs, and sports notables. It is a combination of hard business, motivational presentations, creative thinking and all-round corporate schmoozing at $1500 a table. It also has the trappings of a see-and-be-seen event and will be well attended by some of the people that Peter often bumps up against.

It's not really my cup of tea but I've got a shitload of wine to sell and there's not much I won't do – within reason – to promote the brand.

As you walk from the parking lot to the entrance of Blenheim Airport, there is no doubt that you are in Marlborough wine country. The major wineries are well represented with hoardings along the front façade of the building; among others there are Hunter's, Spy Valley, Montana, Allan Scott, Villa Maria, and the latest addition – Yealands Estate. To the left of the entrance is a statue of viticulture pioneer David Herd. While certainly not a household name, David Herd is a major reason why many people all over the world now enjoy Marlborough wine.

Born in Scotland in 1829, Herd immigrated to Australia in 1852 and after finding the climate there not to his liking he moved on to New Zealand in 1855, settling in Marlborough. After managing the 20,000-acre Meadowbank Station for twenty years he left that job in 1884 to farm

300 acres of land he had earlier purchased in the Fairhall/Brancott area, which later became known as Auntsfield Farm. For the rest of his life Herd worked at his orchards, the cultivation of muscatel grapes and the making of wine. His wine won many prizes at local exhibitions, garnered a good reputation throughout the province and was even recommended by many medical men for its excellent quality. Herd died in 1905, but the winery he established kept producing about 175 gallons of excellent wine annually until 1931 and there are still descendants of his in Marlborough. Although Herd's early viticultural endeavours pre-date the better known introductory work of Romeo Bragato, he remains essentially unknown outside the area and, if truth be told, not much better known in Marlborough.

Peter Yealands probably would have liked David Herd. Herd started with little more than some land and a desire to make something happen. He was mostly self-taught in his winemaking pursuits and trial and error played a large part in his methodology. But equipped with a vision, a penchant for hard work, and the oenologically blessed Marlborough climate, David Herd certainly made something happen. He must be considered the forerunner of the Marlborough wine industry.

Peter takes his place in the customary short queue at the check-in counter, where he meets an acquaintance who is going to the same event and they chat briefly. Peter presents an imposing figure. Now in his early sixties, he is still a strong, burly man, though by his own admission putting on too much weight due to all the office work he has to do now. He is dressed in his usual attire: clean but well-worn Swanndri pullover, work trousers and scuffed boots. He carries the aura of a grizzled old tighthead prop (if you're a rugby person) or a real-time Father Christmas. His flowing white hair and Santa-worthy beard make him immediately recognisable and at the same time somewhat intimidating. There is about him an overall impression of a quiet, powerful man who does not suffer fools gladly, offers little in the way of small talk and would generally rather be somewhere else. This is not to say that he is a crusty old curmudgeon because he's not; once you get by the intimidation factor he has a ready smile, a sincere concern for those he interacts with and is pleasant and very interesting company.

It's only a twenty-five-minute flight to Wellington across the Cook

Strait and the usual aircraft is a Beech 19-seater – that's the one where you have to duck your head getting in and walking to your seat. Peter boards the plane and works his way to the back, takes his seat and soon they're off. The ground falls away and a wider view of the airport and RNZAF Base Woodbourne fans out below. Several passengers immediately point out the rows of mothballed A4 Skyhawks sheathed in white plastic forming a Goliath's toy set on the ground. But they quickly become just another detail in the ever expanding and seemingly boundless sea of green vines that carpet the Wairau Valley.

Soon the plane is swinging east out toward the Cook Strait and Peter has his eyes glued to the window, not unlike a child or first-time flyer. Others may find this somewhat endearing, not realising that while most of us can see everything we own by looking out our front window, Peter is one of those few people who can only see all that is his from the air. He still has three vineyards around Blenheim and his sprawling 2000ha farm in the Marlborough Sounds.

> *After I left the mussel industry, I purchased 5000 acres at Kaiuma Bay in the Sounds and I've planted thousands of trees out there; many showing great autumn colours and also being attractive to native birds and all planted with long-term sustainable forestry farming in mind. I suppose the whole idea of sustainability came about from being at the opposite end of it in my earlier days. Maturity I guess brings some benefits and I don't mind saying that I've been a proper bastard in my time. Many things I used to do, I'd never do now. If we go back to my farming days in the 90s, I've always had a passion for trees, though earlier the passion seemed to be for cutting them down.*

As the plane heads out over Cloudy Bay, the sweep of the Yealands Estate vineyard and winery in Seddon, covering over 1000ha, comes into view to the south. To many the Yealands Estate Winery marks the high point of Peter's business accomplishments and is indeed the reason why he is on his way to an up-market corporate event where he will speak in front of "the suits". But in the career timeline of Peter Yealands, it is simply where he happens to be today. There is much more to the man – as those attending this event will find out.

The plane is soon approaching the ridiculously narrow ribbon of concrete that is Wellington Airport and Peter looks out at the heavy stonework reaching into the water that he and a small crew put in there many years ago. The job was a landmark in his career as it gave him a real indication of the money that could be made with a lot of hard work, a goodly amount of Kiwi know-how, and a healthy indifference to red tape and the orthodox way of doing things.

The plane lands and Peter heads out to the taxi rank. On the drive into town he frets a bit over his upcoming presentation but he knows that this is part of the overall job of marketing the wine and the brand. And there will be some familiar faces: Yealands Estate will have a Cellar Door booth at the event and a corporate table for some of Peter's business acquaintances.

He arrives at the downtown arena where the event is taking place and the taxi drops him at one side of the building. Not unlike a gawking tourist he looks around to see where the entrance is. As he's looking one way and then the other, a fellow in pinstripes with a name-badge dangling from his silk-tied collar walks by, takes one look at him and points to the rear of the building, saying, "The loading door's down that way, mate." Peter laughs and sets off down to the back door, enjoying the joke. One can only imagine the reaction of that well-heeled guide when Peter is introduced later in the morning.

Peter's track record of mingling with the business establishment has been occasionally scratchy, though never confrontational as that's just not his style. Events like this are not usually where he wants to be and in some cases are not places that seem to want him either.

In 2004, at the Romeo Bragato conference in Blenheim, there was a high-end black-tie wine industry event that I really had no choice but to attend, but at least I could take my wife Vai with me so off we go. And this was one of the few times when I actually did put on a jacket and tie, though I can tell you the tie wasn't black. And then this person – must have been a waiter because he was better dressed than me – comes over. I guess he thought we were tourists who had wandered into the wrong room and he asked us to move as the table we'd sat down at was reserved. So we did and sat elsewhere and were told that was reserved as well. By this time I felt like a proper prick standing in the middle of this bloody great room with my wife so in the end I said, "Stuff this, we're out of here," so we went to a restaurant down the road, had a nice meal and went home.

And it's not just the social aspects that can be a nuisance. His well-documented frays with the business establishment over the years have rattled many in the community. But those who judge a man by what he does rather than by what he wears or drives have few problems with Peter Yealands. It was not by chance that he received the first Marine Farm licence for mussel farming in the Marlborough Sounds in the 1970s. It was not just good luck that his Kaiuma Station farm set enviable standards for sustainable forestry resulting in justly recognised conservation awards. It is no accident that he now owns the largest privately owned vineyard in the country with the most environmentally advanced winery in the world. Peter has always been a man of results and though his results speak loudly for themselves, a little help from their creator never hurts and that is why Peter is in Wellington today.

CHAPTER ONE

Tractor-seat Philosophy

I love working my tractors and diggers and I do a lot of thinking out there.

It's a formidable lineup at Thrive Wellington and Peter is scheduled to be the last speaker before lunch. He's a little nervous and perhaps wondering what he's doing here, but after presentations by Peri Drysdale MBE, of Snowy Peak Ltd and Untouched World, and Martin Snedden, CEO of the 2011 Rugby World Cup, it becomes abundantly clear that Peter is in exactly the right place. These too are people who have taken the accepted way of doing things by the scruff of the neck and done things their way, resulting in wonderful accomplishments. And though the host's introduction of Peter might be considered just a wee bit patronising – playing up the work clothes and naming his session Tractor-seat Philosophy – it is obviously sincere and indicative of the Kiwi appreciation for men and women who go out and get the job done.

Peter is not comfortable and it would not be surprising if many of these well-polished folk are anticipating a Country Calendar cocky with mud (or worse) on his boots stammering his way through a pained and halting presentation. He makes no pretence of eloquence or oratorical mastery and as if to confirm their preconceptions he shuffles his notes and clears his throat a couple of times before he starts.

But then he throws them a curve ball and leads off his presentation with a professional and entertaining video that runs regularly in the audio/visual theatre at Yealands Estate Winery. It outlines the far-reaching and innovative processes that are the hallmark of this world-leading production facility and at the same time reinforces Peter's profound love of the land. It tells of the extensive design and implementation of wetlands that abound on the property, attracting many species of birds that are usually not welcome in vineyards. The audience hears of the meticulous planning ensuring the maximum sustainability of the winery, including the use of solar and wind turbine technology, and the recycling of all by-products – most importantly the water. Peter's goal of not only being completely self-powered but eventually contributing electricity back into the power grid is not only suggested but in effect promised. With so many these days talking the talk of ecology and sustainability, it quickly becomes obvious that Peter Yealands is walking the walk, and on an unprecedented scale.

With the end of the video, Peter gets on with his speech and does so the old-fashioned way: he tells them where he came from, what he did, what he's doing and what the future holds for him. And once the style (or lack of) is accepted, the stories that pour forth are enthralling and the audience becomes quieter and quieter because now they don't want to miss a word.

He starts with a genuine and heart-felt chat about his father, Keith, and particularly Keith's wartime exploits in North Africa with the Long Range Desert Group (LRDG). Peter makes no bones about the fact that the motivation and persistence that drive him come from his father. He describes Keith's ability to tackle the hard jobs and, foreshadowing Peter's own proclivity for keeping a lot of balls in the air at the same time, lists the various enterprises that Keith took on simultaneously and successfully. He also proudly points out an upcoming Anzac Day television documentary that will feature the exploits of the LRDG and his father and for just a few moments all the audience sees is a grown-up boy who is very proud of his dad. He describes his early family days in a hard-working environment where everyone mucked in and helped get the work done.

My parents started with nothing, thought anything was possible and proved all was do-able. Business was done with a handshake, the smiles were genuine and the money was real.

Peter moves on to his own endeavours, briefly lamenting that everything he did early on seemed to be a challenge, though he quickly points out the exception to this trend – his forty years of marriage to Vai, his two children and now three grandchildren.

> *In a real sense, I'm a jack-of-all-trades and a master of none. I left school when I was 14 and don't have much in the way of formal qualifications. But I do know what's right and what's wrong, and I'm proud to say that my whole family and I have come through the system without any major skirmishes with the law, without any claims on the country and we're still all here today.*

He goes on to describe some of his early work and one can begin to see a pattern emerge. Peter has never been afraid to take on the hard and challenging work, and though he tells of his enjoyment of doing things that others couldn't or wouldn't do, he's no fool when it comes to business.

He speaks of his early days in the mussel farming industry – and Peter can truly talk of the early days because he was the first in the country to receive a Marine Farming licence. But what many don't realise is that it wasn't just about mussel farming, it was also fabricating all the equipment needed, as there was no established infrastructure or supply chain in New Zealand for this industry. The equipment needed ranged from ferro-cement barges to plastic floats to hold the longlines in the water and these all had to be made pretty much from scratch. And therein lie some stories, as Peter goes on to tell some classic "no. 8 wire" tales involving automobile differentials, agitator washing machines and a large dollop of Kiwi ingenuity in the production of the required equipment.

> *When we started in with the mussel farming, everything was done from rafts – there was no such thing as these longlines hanging from floats that are used today. The rafts started off as these huge ferro-cement things – and that was an interesting project just to make those. And plus the red tape getting them certified was a nightmare, so we were keen to use what the Japanese were using, which were the longlines. So we tried it out, hanging lines from some 44-gallon steel drums, but after a few storms, the bloody things fell to bits and there were these drums running everywhere around the*

Sounds. So I decided there was a need to make plastic floats and that worked out very well for me and I made a lot of floats and a lot of money with them.

Peter told of more exploits, including the Wellington Airport job, and the atmosphere was now that of youngsters gathered around a campfire listening to the old master spinning yarns. Another factor begins to emerge and that is Peter's inherent attitude to risk. We all know the adages concerning risk and reward but very few of us are able to deal with risk the way Peter has.

The important thing about risk is that it must be accepted, respected and accounted for. Just ignoring it is always a recipe for failure.

The key with all of Peter's endeavours has been the rational and pragmatic acceptance of risk, the calculation and consequences of its cost, and the ability to then get on with the job without fear, because the risk has already been thought through and dealt with. It may look like a reckless lack of fear, but it is actually an acceptance of risk without letting it affect the job at hand. He has tackled major projects where the risks have been enormous and his philosophy of planning for and accepting them has been a decisive factor in his success. If he does have a lack of fear it is that he is not afraid to fail, and this combined with his approach to risk have stood him well.

Peter now turned his attention to his involvement in the wine industry.

Over the years I bought a few farms, nine actually, of some 5000 hectares. We've pounded in a million fence posts, planted two million vines, and strung over 22,000km of wire. We've built a winery and are now involved in the marketing and distribution of our wine all over the world. We've got some great people out there and some of the permanent staff people at the winery have been with me all my working life. We also employ a large group of migrant workers every year and we put them up on site. They come from Thailand,

Indonesia and the Pacific Islands and without a word of a lie they're
a pleasure to have. I don't know why we have all this fuss about
seasonal workers. None have ever caused me any trouble.

People are a great asset, and I like people who are honest, hard-
working and fun to be with. I like people who are smarter than me,
who look after their families, and who don't waste money and show
off. With good people around you, you can solve most problems and
I've been blessed with good people around me.

This may sound like a crowd-pleasing platitude, but few in attendance have likely seen the facilities that Peter provides for his people. When
you drive out to Yealands Estate you see a very striking, large, modern
building set among the vineyards just before you reach the winery. Knowing that Peter lives out there, one assumes that this is his house – but it
isn't. His is the modest little farmhouse at the back that came with the
property; the big house you see from the road is for his people. It contains
offices, showers, bunkrooms, a kitchen and smoko – a much bigger and
more modern place than his home.

It's out in the vineyards where Peter lives up to the title of his seg-
ment and becomes the Tractor-seat Philosopher.

I spend a fair bit of time thinking – sometimes at night, but then
I've forgotten most of it by morning, but I do most of my think-
ing when I'm on a tractor or digger. I love my machines and love
shifting the soil and I feel the way a potter or sculptor must feel
taking a raw lump of clay and making something of it. I often miss
my Sunday roasts because I can't get off my machine to get home for
dinner. I've spent thousands of hours working my machines and
I've come up with some great ideas and some bloody loopy ideas. My
point here is that an hour of undistracted thinking time can be very
valuable. My best ideas have come from this special thinking time
and most from the seat of a tractor.

So far it's all been warm and affable yarn spinning; Peter now takes
a more serious tone. The New Zealand share market (NZX) is something

that Peter thinks about from time to time and although this may not be the most receptive group to address on the issue, that is of little concern to him.

There are fewer and fewer things in which people can safely invest. They're driven to the banks and driven to forgetting about any thought of getting capital uplift as well as an income. Companies which need capital cannot get it, and good projects end up being starved of equity capital so consequently they don't grow. We ought to be able to get New Zealand capital for New Zealand projects. Ordinary New Zealand investors should be able to get some capital growth. I do not pretend to know much about these sorts of things, but I do believe that in New Zealand we need better, more positive and safer equity markets.

We also need better policing from those whose task it is to do so. In a small commercial community like New Zealand we should be able to control things better. We should be able to see what's going on, we should know what's going on and we should have watchdogs that can smell trouble and bark when there's trouble about.

I'm hopeful that one day Yealands Estate can be open for public investment to assist me in growing a global distribution network. My aim is in five years to be one of the top five wineries in New Zealand, and following that the best in New Zealand, and I will need help to get there.

Peter then speaks of his belief in sustainability:

I've become a convert to sustainability. I know that in the past I've done some bloody stupid things to the environment so I'm very much driven by sustainability. I believe that when we've all done our time on this planet, we should leave behind a good place for our children and grandchildren. We should leave some wood in the hut so to speak. We should leave some rivers for them to admire and play in and fish in. We should leave some birds to sing for them.

As to the future, I like the words "looking forward". They give me feelings of optimism and excitement. There is the challenge of meet-ing what's round the corner and the excitement of meeting new people each day. 2008 has been a tough year and 2009 is likely going to be tougher, but let's not be negative. With our Kiwi "no. 8 wire" approach and our resilience, we will succeed. So let's not be afraid to fail and let's celebrate our successes, let's applaud our young innovators, let's be courageous and bold and let's look after our patch as best we can.

With that Peter is done; his candid honesty is well appreciated and he receives a warm accolade. Later he took part in a round-table forum where a lot of the talk was about the people you work with. When asked whether he felt he was taking a chance hiring a young local winemaker to manage such a daunting enterprise, Peter replied that he felt that his winemaker, Tamra Washington, was taking a chance on him. He reiterated his earlier comments on the strength and importance of those who work for you and that he is always looking for the best people he can find. Walking about the venue after Peter's presentation, many are chatting about what they've just heard. A little bit of wonder at the intriguing stories is mixed with the realisation that they have heard a remarkable man speaking straight from the heart.

With Peter Yealands there is always the underlying feeling that he is not quite normal, that he is an anomaly and perhaps even a little strange. He obviously doesn't look the part here – with the casual attire, the long hair and beard. But there is nothing counter-culture about him. And while he may describe himself as a jack-of-all-trades, his many endeavours have consistently proved that he is a master jack-of-all-trades. And as with any good story, the subject begets many questions. Why does he inspire such unabashed loyalty in those who work for him and with him? Why do some in the business establishment fear him, loathe him and/or decline to take him seriously? Why does the man take on challenging projects when he knows little of the nuts and bolts of that particular field? And most importantly, why and how does he succeed? A lot of it has to do with where he came from and Peter has always been the first to acknowledge that among other things, he is truly his father's son.

CHAPTER TWO

A Kiwi Scorpion

Dad's a battler and he taught me everything I know.

LRDG – OPERATION CARAVAN: On 1 September 1942, Trooper Keith Yealands of T1 Patrol was in his customary spot at the back of a heavily modified 30cwt Chevrolet truck, where he and Sandy Sanders manned a tripod-mounted Breda machine gun. The Long Range Desert Group (LRDG) had just set off on a mission from their base at Fayoum, 130km southwest of Cairo, just west of the Nile in Egypt. The LRDG has become almost mythical in New Zealand military history and was the forerunner of the better-known SAS of the British and Commonwealth forces. The group's main job throughout the war in Africa was surveillance, intelligence gathering and charting and comprised those who had answered a call for men "…who do not mind a hard life, scanty food, little water, lots of discomfort, and possess stamina and initiative". Small wonder that the majority of LRDG's manpower were Kiwis who were used to living in relative isolation with their customary "she'll be right", can-do attitude and the ability to improvise and work on their own.

Each patrol was a self-contained, independent unit capable of travelling hundreds of kilometres deep into enemy territory and, just as importantly, getting back again over the very difficult desert terrain, which included the ever-shifting and dangerous Sand Sea. These tough, self-reliant men, who had adapted to desert life with its extreme climatic and geographical conditions, became known as the Kiwi Scorpions and every now and then they liked to show their sting. This mission was going to do just that: this was going to be more than watching and reporting. It was going to be a genuine "beat-up", as they called it, where they would have a chance to get out the heavy ordnance and have a go against the enemy.

If Charles Dickens had been writing a century later, he would have been half right – it was the worst of times. Europe essentially belonged to Hitler and the heroic yet denigrating spectacle of Dunkirk had been permanently etched into the collective memory of the Allies. Just a month earlier, in August 1942, an Allied mission to determine the actual strength of German defences on the English Channel resulted in a Canadian task force getting badly mauled at Dieppe. It was yet another brave fiasco and it left the Axis confident in the knowledge that "Fortress Europe" had been established. They were now looking further afield to secure footholds outside of Europe and the bellicose glare of their attention fell squarely on North Africa.

The strategic benefits were obvious: it would provide virtually total control of the Mediterranean and the jewel at its eastern end, the Suez Canal, and of course oil. The British Empire had a long and difficult history in the area, from the heroically flamboyant exploits of T.E. Lawrence (of Arabia) to the rather murky redrawing of the Middle-Eastern map after World War I resulting in frictions that continue still. But it was British turf so to speak and any Axis efforts to gain control of the area would be met with stiff and knowledgeable resistance. And if Egypt was in the British sphere, Italy held similar sway in Libya and what was then Tripolitania.

LRDG – OPERATION CARAVAN: On that September morning, though most of them didn't yet know it, the LRDG troopers were on their way to Barce (*ph.* bar-chay), an Italian-held town some 1850km behind enemy lines, where there was an aerodrome vital to the Axis supply lines. Barce was an integral part of Rommel's arena, which stretched from Benghazi to Tobruk, but the Allied strategic wheels were turning. The British were in the midst of their planning for the El Alamein attack and a raid on the Barce aerodrome, code-named Operation Caravan, was planned as a simultaneous subsidiary action of Operation Bigamy, aimed at Benghazi. Their orders were "To raid Barce town and aerodrome causing the maximum amount of damage and disturbance to the enemy". A "beat-up" indeed, but for security reasons only the patrols' officers were aware of the mission.

There would be a lot of other Allied traffic along the coast toward Tobruk and Benghazi, so the LRDG was given an alternate route much further south, which would require two crossings of the Sand Sea. They were on their own with thirty days of fuel and provisions, over dangerous terrain occupied by the enemy, and probably couldn't be happier. An old newspaper clipping dated 14 March 1941 tells how these Kiwi Scorpions felt about their duty:

> It is not just the "highwayman" tactics that appeals to them, but the fact that the men were able to make the journey at all over such hazardous country. Free and easy it may be to these gallant men, but there is a quality of daredevil romance in the exploits of this group, which thrills the imagination in these days when warfare has become only grim and horrible.

Keith Yealands had only recently joined the LRDG. He answered a call for volunteers and was one of only forty selected from 800 men. Nicknamed Junior, as he had joined with his brother Ken and was both younger and smaller, it was a long road that brought him to this time and place. In 2009 Keith spoke of his background and his recollections of his wartime service:

> As far as I know, I was born in Blenheim – in 1921, I know that. I don't know where Mum was born. I never ever knew my father; he deserted the family when I was born. I was the youngest of six and at one stage I was farmed out, passed around the family, and then I knocked around up north for a bit before the war, in Gisborne and Auckland. Did some shearing, weeding strawberries, whatever I could find. I'd left school at thirteen and I worked in town here in Blenheim out at Rapaura on a dairy farm for a while before I went up North. It was hard times; I carried the swag and slept out rough between rolls. Then I went to Auckland and I worked at Turners and Growers, who were produce merchants. They made a great fuss of me there. I think they felt sorry for me because I was a

little fella and so young, living out on my own in a single room,
nowhere to cook anything, only seven shillings a week and
most of it went on room rent. And then in 1939 the war started
and I wanted to be part of it. I went back to Blenheim and of
course I was underage – many were – but I got Mum to sign
a letter saying it was okay. She wasn't too happy about it I can
tell you but she gave me the letter to say I had her permission. I
joined the 23rd Infantry Battalion and we trained some in New
Zealand and then I was off to England.

When they arrived in England, Keith found himself in Tunbridge
Wells working as a driver for the liaison officers between the New Zealand and English forces. He was stationed miles away from his original
group and had little to do with his own battalion at first, but they were
soon shifted out and on their way to Egypt. Only three days later they left
for the Greek campaign. When they were ordered to walk out of Greece
on a night march Keith turned his ankle badly and when he told his supe-
rior officer he couldn't walk, the officer said, "Well you either walk or stay
here and be a prisoner, please yourself." Keith walked and when they got
to Crete he was put in hospital.

Then the Germans started to fly over; they'd come low over
the hospital and you could hear the bombs. There was a lot of
talk of invasion and I thought well hospital's no place to be so I
got my gear and walked out. I couldn't go back to my regiment
– I'd have been in trouble for leaving without a discharge – so
I scouted round and found the Divisional Cavalry. Parts of
them were still in Crete and parts of them had been put onto
a different ship and gone to Egypt. I found the blokes camped
out in an olive grove and found the commanding officer, Major
John Russell, and told him who I was. He said, "All right if you
are as good as your brother, you can be my runner." So I was his
runner.

The German paratroopers invaded a few days after I left
the hospital. I remember we were all lined up for breakfast one

morning with our mess tins and these planes came over and blokes started jumping out of them. So I dropped my breakfast, rushed back to my cot for my rifle and went into action straight away. It was the first time that I fired, actually shot at anyone, and I got in a good shooting. From then on it was every day, and more German paratroopers kept coming in. The ones that landed on top of us were shot at so they started landing down the valley a bit and then came up and attacked us. I guess you could say we were finally chased out and were evacuated back to Egypt.

I was still with Major Russell. Good bloke and I liked working for him so I stayed with the Div Cav when we got back to Egypt and fought in the desert campaign. After one particular go there in the desert they decided that they would toughen up a bit on discipline. When you come out of action like that they usually gave you a bit of time off, no parades, that sort of thing. But they decided they would sweat the beer out of us and called a group march and of course I piped up and said, "I can't march, I've got a bad ankle." I don't think they really believed me, but they sent me off to field hospital, x-rayed it and said, "Oh, you do have a bad ankle after all," and sent me off to rest camp in Alexandria. I was bored out of my mind there so I did a gunnery instructor course and I passed that and did quite well, finishing at the top. So they decided to send me back to New Zealand as an instructor, but I didn't want to come home – I wasn't ready. Then they called for volunteers for the LRDG so I volunteered for that and got accepted, much to everybody's surprise.

LRDG – OPERATION CARAVAN: By 11am, 13 September, T1 patrol had reached a point just 24km from Barce and were preparing for their final approach. It had been a long and difficult trek and they were already shy of some men and equipment due to accidents. Planning for their return, they had set up rendezvous points with provisions at various locations. This was standard procedure, as getting back was just as important as getting there, but it meant that what they now carried was only enough for the raid itself and supplies for a few days. At dusk they set off and by midnight the raid was on.

An ensuing mishap put Junior's truck out of action and he was now with Merlyn Craw in the tail-end vehicle following the others onto the airfield. He and Craw took their hand-made bombs, jumped off the truck and ran to a target aircraft, set the short fuses and quickly got back in the truck for the run-up to the next target. The surprise factor soon expired and the Italians were returning fire with machine guns and mortars and the airfield became an arena of bullets, bombs and cross-fire, but Craw and Yealands still managed to destroy ten aircraft with no injury to themselves. The raid itself was a spectacular success: destroyed and burning enemy aircraft littered the field and the sting of the Kiwi Scorpions had proved to be devastatingly effective. But the wounded enemy's blood was up and bent on retaliation; it was time to get out of town. And it would not be easy. "Getting out was a bugger," recalls Keith.

> Me and Merlyn had lost our truck and went up the road on foot with our Thompson's [machine guns]. We came up to a corner and there was a dirty great armoured car fair and square in our way blocking us, so we went past him at a good clip, went up the road, stopped and had a look around and couldn't see any opposition up there or anything and nobody seemed to have even missed us. But Merlyn said we had better go back and have another go so we turned round and went back. As we came into it I was busy firing at the armoured car that had moved over to the other corner – and that's when I got hit; that's the last I remember.

Yealands had taken a rifle shot to the back of his head and fell into the back of a burning truck. Trooper Ewan Hay had been in that truck and was dazed and bloodied from the crash. When he came to he saw Junior's legs sticking out the back. He lurched up to the blazing vehicle to pull Yealands out but was grabbed from behind by Italian soldiers. With a pistol pressed into his back, Hay raised his hands while trying to explain that a man had to be rescued. The Italians understood and let Hay approach the truck and pull Yealands from the flames. Unconscious, severely wounded and close to death, Yealands was now a POW. He was taken to a hospital, where he was thrown in a corner, medically ignored and essentially left to die.

The Barce raid was deemed a success and achieved the objectives of the mission. And though many were wounded and taken prisoner and much equipment was destroyed, the LRDG's efforts compromised the enemy's defences and caused significant disruption and redeployment of much needed resources, which would have a positive result in the El Alamein campaign. But for Trooper Keith Yealands the future looked bad and short.

> I remember lying somewhere and I couldn't see, couldn't hear, couldn't speak and I just didn't know what the hell was going on. Then I heard someone asking me what my name was. I couldn't answer him and I couldn't see him, but I felt him give me a jab in the leg and I came round and I was in an Italian hospital. They gave me a hiding, beat me up, not badly because it knocked me out. But when I came around they were standing there looking at me and one of them leant over and he said, "Are you an American?" "No, not American, a New Zealander." So he hit me and then they all gave me a bit of a punch and they got a few blows but not many because they knocked me out again. It didn't hurt much and then the other blokes, the other prisoners started saying, "When are you going to do something for him? Why don't you do something for him?" Ah, he'll die soon was the reply. They left me for five days but I wasn't ready to die. No I wasn't. They finally gave me something to eat. I hadn't anything to eat since the raid and I'd been going on my hands and knees for water. I remember that – I remember crawling for water. Each time they'd look at me – just waiting for me to die. Anyway they took me away and shaved my head and that was painful so I abused them, swore at them, called them filthy names and when they'd finished the

nurse gave me a glass of brandy, quite a jolt of brandy as I recall. I drank it and she said all better now.

A few days later they took me down to a hospital boat across to Naples and then to the prisoner of war hospital in Naples. I think it was four months in that hospital and then on to a POW camp in Udine in northern Italy. I was there for what must have been eight months or so altogether. Then one night I heard a lot of commotion, people yelling, and when I got up in the morning we were surrounded by a heavy cordon of German troops. So they marched us out of the camp the same day on to a train, and I spent three days on that bloody train whittling open the door through the lock so a couple of us could get out. But the rest of the mob wouldn't let us go. They had been told that the Germans would fire, there would be reprisals, and any attempt at escape they'd fire on us. We were three days in that bloody train. They took us to a POW camp [Stalag VIII-A, east of Görlitz, now Zgorzelec, Poland], which had Russian prisoners and we were there for two or three weeks. I think we were well treated, better than the rest of them. They put us in a special barracks just outside the main camp but we used to see them wheeling the dead out every morning in hand-carts. They'd make two or three trips with three or four bodies on the hand-cart out to a big trench and just throw them in. Then they put us back on a train and took us to somewhere in Germany and had us working in a coalmine. It was a bloody deep mine, some 1500 metres deep, and we worked a twelve-hour day, every day. I started to have blackouts there so they sent me off to a specialist in the town. He told me that I had something stuck in my brain but it was in too deep to get out so he gave me a note to say that I wasn't to work underground. So I got back to camp with this note and went to work up top but the Germans looked at me and said, "Oh no we'll send you to a shallow mine." So they sent me to some other place in Poland. I don't know how long we were in Poland – quite a long while it seemed. Then they came in one morning; it was raining and cold and they said we were moving out in an hour. So we had to get what we could carry and they marched us off then and I remember it was in January – must have been January '45.

We marched through that winter and spring into Czechoslovakia. We were marching one evening and I said to my mate Bob Haydon, "What'ya reckon, let's get outta here. All we have to do is walk out the front gate when they're herding the mob." They used to put us in barns to sleep so on a rest day just on dusk we saw the Germans herding everyone back into the barn so Bob and I just walked down the path and walked out the gate. But they picked us up the next day and that was our fault because we were starving. The only reason we escaped was to go to the Czech civilians to try and get something to eat because the Germans fed us bugger-all. We knew we couldn't go anywhere because we didn't even know where we were. We knew we were in Czechoslovakia but which way was out?

When the next prisoner convoy came through, they put us with that one and by this time we could hear gunfire. We still didn't know quite where we were but we'd been told they were taking us to Austria. So one day in one of the barns I found a container of potatoes and Bob and I spent the day mashing potatoes up, squeezing the juice out of them till we had made a thick, dirty great sausage, wrapped it up in my singlet, and we reckoned we could go now because we had something to eat for a few days. And when we were marching that night I said to Bob, "You walk right behind me and when I go you step out and follow me." So I stepped off into the trees and Bob went walking behind me but he must have been half asleep because he didn't walk quietly and he fell over some bloody logs and dropped his bucket. So they started to chase us and fired at us but they didn't make much of an effort to catch us. I think we were another five days getting across country and still had the food – we'd held on to that.

We were waiting at a bend in the road and wondering

whether to wait for dark before we crossed or give it a bit of
a run. But then we heard vehicles and saw half-tracks coming
down towards us. I'd never seen a half-track before and didn't
know whose they were – ours or theirs. But when it came
closer, there was a star on it, an American star. So I jumped up
and just about got shot, but the Yanks figured we were okay
and they put us in one of those each. Bob in one and me in the
other. We stayed with them for about three weeks and found
out we were back in Germany. The Americans were awfully
good to us, cigarettes and food, couldn't do enough, but we
could see they didn't really want us around too much longer;
asked us to piss off actually, but were decent enough about
it. So one day we saw a truck parked at a house, found it was
workable and we drove away.

And drive away they did. They headed generally north and west
and found themselves in Brussels on VE day, 8 May 1945, and by all
accounts had a wonderful time there. The Belgians were very appreciative
of Allied soldiers and though Keith and Bob must have looked like a pair
of ragamuffins, they spoke the right language and so they enjoyed the
Belgian hospitality. They finally hitched a ride on a Stirling bomber back
to England and found themselves in Margate. Keith and Bob wallowed
in the relative luxury of England and actually volunteered to go back to
Europe as interpreters as they had both picked up enough German to
qualify, but Keith's health conditions put an end to any more active duty
and it was time to go home.

His journey from near-death to victory celebrations had spanned
almost three years. He had endured a near-fatal gunshot wound, beat-
ings, hundreds of miles of forced marches, slave-labour in coalmines,
and escapes from his captors. He still carried shell fragments in his head,
which would compromise his health for the rest of his life, but Keith
was nowhere near done. It was 1945 and he was twenty-four – an age
when most young men are just getting started and thinking about a job or
perhaps getting married. He had already lived through experiences most
of us can't begin to comprehend. He had seen the worst of men and the

best of men, and his rock-hard bloody-minded perseverance had seen him through. Now it was time to get on with the rest of his life.

Back Home

In 1945, Blenheim was a small town servicing the various rural activities of Marlborough. This was well before its current role as hub of the booming Marlborough wine industry and at that time it was chiefly sheep and dairy farming and orchards. Doris Davies had been born in Nelson in 1923 and she and her family shifted to Blenheim in the late 20s. She attended school there and by her account spent a normal childhood and teenage years until the war started. Things changed then, with an influx of soldiers and many airmen from the nearby Woodbourne base. Dorrie, as she was called, remembers the dances.

> It seemed as though there were dances every night and we quite enjoyed it all. I didn't see anyone in particular on a regular basis; I guess because no one was there for too long. We wrote letters to many of our local fighting boys as well. Not those weepy soppy sorts of letters, just nice letters letting them know what was going on back home and that we were all thinking of them. As the war went on, we were all expected to chip in and do our bit. I went to work at the Ritz restaurant waiting tables and helping out as there were lots of customers then, just about all servicemen.

The Ritz, now long gone, was run by Keith's mother and his sister Daphne and in late 1945 talk turned to Keith's imminent return from the war. Dorrie remembers that Keith's mum knew he'd been wounded and had been a POW and was worried that she might not recognise him. They had heard the stories of men returning home horribly scarred and disfigured from war wounds and as they had no firm details, they could only prepare for the worst. In August, Keith's troopship arrived in Wellington, where he promptly caught the ferry to Picton, took the bus into Blenheim, and walked into the Ritz, bumping into a pretty waitress at the front door. After the usual coming-home rituals with his mum and sister,

Keith's attention returned to the pretty waitress and he asked her out that evening. Keith recalls, "I had a fair bit of heavy courting to do. The next morning Mum asked where we'd gone and I said the pub. And then I said I'm going to marry that girl and three months later we were married."

Keith had the task of finding work, especially now that he was a married man with responsibilities, and find work he did, beginning his remarkable career as a businessman that would ultimately result in his being awarded an OBE. And while all that was going on, Keith and Dorrie also got down to the other business of starting and raising a family. Susan was born in 1947, the twins Kevin and Stephen were born in 1952, and in between, in May 1948, Peter Wayne Yealands was born. This is Peter's story.

CHAPTER THREE

Packhorse Pete

"I'd say, 'You know, Pete, that might not work,' and he'd always say,
'I'll show you'." – Keith Yealands

Keith and Dorrie were married in December 1945. They lived with
Keith's mum at first as she had rooms in her house on Bomford
Street in Blenheim. Dorrie continued working at the Ritz and Keith
found a job truck driving for Marlborough Transport for £7 a week. It
doesn't sound like a lot now but it was a living wage for the times. Keith
stayed at this for a while but he was still suffering from his war wounds,
which made it difficult to handle the truck and loads. In 1947, he bought
a rotary hoe and did some contracting, hiring out for 10 shillings an hour.
But his war wounds still affected him: he'd lost a lot of his reflexes and
couldn't use his hands well and eventually ended up in hospital for over
a month. The doctors did what they could and finally said he could go
home but he would have to sell the hoe and find easier work.

So home he went, sold the hoe and was again looking for work. It
had only been a few months since their first child, Sue, was born and
things weren't looking too promising for the young family. Shortly after
Keith got home from hospital, an insurance agent from Mutual Life called
around to see if they wanted to buy life insurance now that they were
starting a young family. Keith and Dorrie knew they couldn't afford the
insurance but Keith reckoned he could probably sell it. He was restricted
to light work and he thought this would be a good fit. Selling was still
done primarily through direct agents of the insuring company and Keith
soon caught on with Mutual. And he did quite well selling insurance:

Dorrie recalls that Keith won a trip to Wellington for a dinner put on for the top ten agents in the country.

After Peter was born in 1948, Keith stayed on with Mutual Life for a while longer. But he had always aspired to owning his own business and perhaps with memories of that "dirty great sausage" of potatoes that had nourished him during his escape in the war he decided to get into the grocery business. With the help of his brother Ken, who came over from Wellington, Keith built a grocery store on Lee Street in Blenheim. The store, no bigger than a small house with an adjacent storage shed, would establish Keith and set the groundwork for his remarkable business career. It was a small beginning but the business soon became a full-fledged grocery store, buying large quantities in bulk and continuing to expand. The store motto was "Your money buys more at the Lee Street store" and Keith was ahead of his time putting out leaflets that the kids delivered, advertising daily and weekly specials. About a year after the store was opened, Keith built a house adjoining the shop. The grocery store was the major part of the family's lives for many years and provided a stable and comfortable living for them.

Pete's twin brothers Kevin and Stephen came along in 1952. They were very premature – Stephen was only 2¼ lb and Kevin 2¾ lb. Lack of oxygen to the brain was a common problem with premature babies and the prevailing medical opinion at the time dictated that both boys be administered oxygen. Unfortunately prolonged use of oxygen at higher than normal levels can induce oxygen toxicity and one of the conditions it sometimes causes is myopia, which was the case with Stephen, who has had to wear glasses all his life. The twins would remain sickly through much of their early childhood and garnered the lion's share of their parents' time and concern.

Blenheim in the 1950s was the quintessential "sleepy little town". The population in 1951 was barely 7000 and sheep and dairy farming and stone fruit orchards were the main sources of employment and income. The town, like all others everywhere, was still recovering from the war: rationing was still a fact of life for many and of course young families were being started. But the town was growing and over the next ten years the population would increase to 12,000 and the rate of manufacturing would rise by 25 per cent. Many companies that are still in business in Blenheim today were evident, such as Cuddon's, Thomas's, Farmers and Pyne Gould Guinness. In 1954, Thomas P. Shand was the first local MP in fifty years to become a Cabinet Minister and held several different portfolios in the Holyoake government. The same year saw one of the most anticipated events in New Zealand's history, with a visit from Queen Elizabeth – although as the *Marlborough Express* reported many ardent townspeople were "bitterly disappointed" due to a last-minute change from an open to a closed vehicle. Catching a glimpse of the Queen and Prince Philip was almost impossible. "We waited for hours," said one woman, "and you couldn't see a thing. I think they should have used an open car like they'd promised."

The *Marlborough Express*, long the voice of the region, contained many of the usual parochial articles that were standard fare for the times. In 1957 much was made of Prime Minister Holyoake's visit to the annual A&P Show, and in 1959, 6000 people congregated on the Taylor River bank for the town's centenary, presided over by Governor-General Lord Cobham. For those who liked to travel a bit further afield, the new Pelorus Bridge was built in 1956 and greatly eased the trip to Nelson. Numerous building projects were proposed and initiated during 1958 and the now ubiquitous parking meter made its greedy debut on Blenheim streets in January. For all the royal watchers, February was a banner month and they gathered in Market Place to catch a glimpse of the Queen Mother as she made a brief two-hour visit. And the paper reported on the diligent work of Mr. A.H. MacQueen, who attended to the clock in the Seymour Square war memorial tower, tirelessly winding it twice each week. Many new buildings were proposed during these years, including a new girls' college, a co-ed college hostel, a new police station, a college at Woodbourne, new RSA rooms and a Marlborough Harbour Board office. It was also proposed to make a diversion to take Wairau River flood water from Botham's Bend to the sea, and to build a road from Rarangi to White's Bay. In 1958 building started on the first Blenheim motel, and a new traffic bridge over the Wairau River, part of the Nelson-Blenheim highway, was opened by the chairman of the National Roads Board. May featured grand openings, with ribbons being cut at the new Baptist Church on High Street and the new public library in Seymour Square. September was a highlight for the sports minded, with an international hockey game drawing a good crowd to Lansdowne Park on 6 September, though sadly the test between Australia and New Zealand was won by Australia 3–2. And in November the new swimming pool was opened to the public.

It was in this thriving atmosphere that Keith's Lee Street grocery store flourished. Keith didn't think small, often buying by the truckload or boat-load. Bulk packaging required a huge amount of work, getting things broken down to smaller sizes and placing them on the shelves of the store, and this was often part of Pete's chores during his childhood.

Cargo transport in and out of Blenheim was quite different then and it was a local joke that if Picton was the front door to Marlborough, Blenheim was the tradesman's entrance. Until the Wellington to Picton ferry service was established, there was commercial water transport in and out of Blenheim. Back in the 1950s visitors to Blenheim who happened to be in the right place at the right time would be startled to see a ship apparently making its way across a paddock and disappearing among the trees. But to locals it was nothing unusual: it was just the scow AS *Echo* making its way up the twisting and narrow Opawa River to the Park Terrace wharf in the centre of the town. For sixty years the little ship was a lifeline between Blenheim and Wellington. Despite storms and the difficulties of the Wairau Bar she always arrived sooner or later. Customers of the local shops were familiar with the fluctuating timetable of the *Echo* being an excuse for the lack of commodities and the non-arrival of ordered goods.[1]

Peter certainly got to know the *Echo* well, making countless trips hauling the bulk items Keith had ordered for the store. And the work had only started. Once he got everything back to the store, there would be lots

---

1. An interesting note is that during World War II, *Echo* was requisitioned by the US Navy for service in the Pacific, where she rescued many downed American aircraft crews and carried Allied troops. She is thought to have helped track down two Japanese submarines and her story was told, though mostly in caricature, in the 1961 movie *The Wackiest Ship in the Army*, starring Jack Lemmon and Ricky Nelson. After the war she returned to Cook Strait service until 1965, and though still seaworthy became uneconomic due to competition from the ferries. The *Echo* is now in permanent dry dock in Picton and is a popular café and bar.

more to do and most of it was heavy manual labour or tiresome and repet-
itive donkey work. But that's the way things were and one outcome of all
this was the evolution and reason for his nickname when he was young,
"Packhorse Pete". He'd always been big for his age and with all the heavy
physical work he was doing he had become very strong and well built.

*Even when I was a young boy in the grocery shop I used to carry full
sacks of spuds and these sacks were 150lbs. I could have used a sack
barrow but I guess I was a bit of a show-off, and unfortunately it
didn't do my back any good and I'm paying a bit for it now. Speaking of spuds, it was always me. The old man would fill the whole
shed up with spuds and they'd grow eyes and it was my job to de-
sprout the bastards and then re-bag them. I'd spend hours and hours
doing that and then put them into sugar bags, which is how they
were sold in the store.*

Peter was always looking for work opportunities. If he had a few
hours to spare he'd look for a job to fill that time in, so right from the
start he always had several jobs. When he was a youngster he had lawn-
mowing rounds, delivered posters and hand bills, was always working.

*I didn't know anything different – Dad was working all the time,
and not just at the grocery store, so it's just what we did. From when
I was seven or eight I'd be working in the grocery store after school
and on weekends. As I got older I learned to do more things but it
started with breaking up big blocks of dates and putting them into
one pound packets, cracking walnuts, weighing up flour and sugar
and the like. All of those shitty jobs. It was all bulk back then and
that's how Dad bought everything. Then when I was old enough to
serve at the counter I did that and helped out with deliveries as well.
We had a big push-bike with a trailer behind it and we had a pretty
big area to cover. Dad was a very good grocer so we had customers all
over town. Then I got my licence to drive a van and Dad had bought
a brand-new Ford 10 van and I did a lot of the delivery work.*

Peter's brother Kevin's first memories are also of the store.

[Dad] used to buy potatoes by the railway car – came from down South. But before he'd buy them, he'd get a sample, cook them and eat them. If they were good he'd buy them. He never bought a big consignment of potatoes without doing that. As kids, he'd have us out dropping off leaflets all over town describing that week's specials. Most things were bought in bulk back then – honey was in a big container and you'd bring in your own jar or whatever and fill it up in the store. I think he was the first grocer in town to stock Birdseye frozen food.

On summer weekends the family would often go camping in the Marlborough Sounds. Keith and Dorrie would pack all the kids into the delivery van and head off to one of their favourite spots at Moenui Bay, just east of Havelock. Keith eventually bought a section and built a bach there and these were golden days for the family. Peter still remembers catching 20lb snapper from the beach. He was always nagging his dad to let him take their little boat out and Keith would say, "When you can swim, you can take the boat out." But Pete kept on and on about the boat until finally Keith said can you swim and Peter said yes. So Keith and Peter got in the boat, went out a few hundred yards and Keith asked him again, "Can you swim?" – "Yes, Dad, I can swim" and Keith promptly tipped Peter into the water and said, "If you can swim back to shore, you can take the boat out." Peter actually wasn't much of a swimmer, but he flailed about and got headed in the right direction and then found that he could actually touch bottom, though he didn't let on to his dad and finally made it to shore. And so began Peter's lifelong love affair with boats.

While the grocery business was thriving and providing a good living for the family, Keith was always looking for new opportunities. Blenheim was growing quickly and he saw the need and the potential profitability of more housing. Property was still relatively cheap and in the late 50s Keith started buying sections and building flats. The idea and basic design of the flats were Dorrie's and they pioneered the now common practice of building two flats on one section. Keith bought and financed the sections and with a mate who was a carpenter they built the flats and split the profit. Peter recalls helping out with the construction when he was still in school – usually doing the dull hard-labour chores around the worksite. But it gave him a good idea of the basics of construction and instilled a healthy respect for the rewards of opportunity and innovation that would drive his own business endeavours.

When my father was building the flats he had Mike Hill, a local lawyer in town, draw up some legislation that enabled Dad to do cross-rentals – the first cross-rentals done in New Zealand I think – and it would allow two owners with a flat each to gain virtual title on a 999-year lease on a single section. Every block was on a corner site and Dad did fourteen twin units around town – still some there. On weekends, I was the mixer boy with the concrete and also passed the concrete blocks to the bloke doing the block laying. Very hard physical work.

Keith remembers that Peter was a strong-willed young boy who was a great help with the grocery business and later with the building. But Peter and school just didn't mix and in 1962 the constant friction came to a head. The continual scrapes he was getting himself into had come to Keith's attention and it was thought that the best solution for everybody was for Peter to leave school. Though only fourteen, he was a big strong lad and had he remained at school both Keith and Pete knew there would be trouble.

I left school when I was fourteen. Dad was pretty bloody crook and I think the school was quite happy to see me go. This was at Marlborough College back in the co-ed days and I was the youngest person in my class as I'd skipped through a couple of years. I did well at school but had little interest. I was very good at commercial practice – working in the shop after school – but I was a shit-stirrer and got into a lot of mischief.

One night, me and a couple of mates got up onto the roof of the college. We climbed up between two buildings which were only a few feet apart and got up using our feet on one wall and backs on the other wall and scrambled up to the roof. And then once we got up, we had to walk along the front of the college on a big parapet – pretty foolhardy and dangerous looking back on it. We got round to the front and I hung a huge sign I'd made over the front of the building which was a skull and crossbones, like a pirates' flag or the warning on a poison bottle. There was a prefect there whose nick-name was "Skulls" and he was a fair arsehole and picked on me a lot. I was pretty sure he knew about the nickname, and I know every-body else did so I thought I was being pretty clever. Anyway the next morning the fire brigade and police were there – the fire brigade were called to get the sign down. They had a fair idea who did it but they couldn't pinpoint us.

Me and another bloke Roger were the most caned students at college and we used to try and outdo one another to see who would get caned the most. One day the sports teacher – short little bugger and a bit of an upstart – and remember I was big for my age, and he used to pick on me like hell. One day he was caning us and the most you could get was "six of the best" across your arse. And this prick intentionally missed my arse and every stroke was lower down on my bare legs. Well, I stood there and took those six but as soon as he was done, I lost it. I grabbed the cane and smashed it, got in his face and said, "Do that again and I'll f**kin thump ya." I was 5'10" and pretty much fully grown and I think he knew that I probably could thump him.

The final straw involved a pet magpie that Pete would occasionally bring to school. The bird's wings had been clipped and it was a favourite not just with Pete but with the other kids as well. One day when he'd brought it to school he was sitting at the back of the class when the magpie started whistling. Pete and the other kids thought this was pretty neat but the teacher was not impressed and wanted to know who was whistling. There was the usual classroom reaction, with everyone looking anywhere except at the teacher, until the giggling started. This promptly set the magpie off again and the culprit was identified. The teacher started down the aisle toward Pete and said if the bird made one more noise – and at this point the magpie again whistled – it was going out the window. They happened to be in a second-storey classroom and Pete was having none of it and told the teacher that if the bird went out the window, the teacher would be following it. Needless to say he was sent out, magpie in tow, but instead of adding more canings to his "beat Roger" campaign he just kept walking and Pete's school days were pretty much done.

Keith soon had a visit from a chap at the Education Department but he dug in his heels. He told him that if Pete stayed on, he'd end up with a chip on his shoulder or someone might get hurt. He's working for me and he'll stay working for me, Keith said. Luckily the fellow understood the situation and told Keith if he'd send Peter back to school for a fortnight he'd arrange the papers to properly release him. And so it was done. He went to work full time for Keith in the grocery store and building the flats and Peter Yealands began his working life.

Lifelong friend and business colleague Peter Radich made some interesting comments recently about Peter's lack of education:

Peter is one of those very intelligent people who hasn't been "spoiled" by education and so has no real idea of what can and can't be done. His mind is still free and wide-ranging and has never really been fenced in. This has allowed him to venture into areas where more prudent people wouldn't go. This coupled with an absolute lack of fear, including the fear of failing, has done him well. I've occasionally noticed a bit of self-consciousness from him about his lack of formal educa-tion but most people who work with him forget all that very quickly when they see his capacity for getting the job done. I sometimes think that in some ways he would have benefited from advanced education and I wonder what he might have accomplished as an engineer or architect or the like. But then it might have ruined him as well and he seems to be doing just fine the way he is.

School's Out

Keith's health continued to be a worry. The shell fragments in his head were causing all sorts of trouble, including seizures and numbness in his hands, and he had recently been diagnosed with stomach ulcers. Dorrie recalls that he would start in the grocery store as early as four in the morning, work there all day and then he'd be off building the flats in the evenings. It was not the best regime and his health was paying the price with the ulcers and then the first of many heart attacks. Dorrie was worried about him but she had been kept busy both with the family and keeping an eye on the grocery store while Keith recovered – although now he was out of school Peter was able help more with both the grocery store and the construction work. The store was thriving, the flats were soon all sold and by now Keith had bought six houses that he was renting out, bringing in a decent income. But the toll on his health was just too much and it was time for a change – doctor's orders, and probably Dorrie's as well. So in 1963 Keith put the grocery store on the market, where it sold quickly and for a very good price. Though it was obviously a good and necessary move for Keith, Peter was a little disappointed.

> *I was a bit pissed about that because I really liked the business but I was obviously far too young to step into the management of the store. Dad had built the grocery store up to a very good business and was the longest-serving grocer in Marlborough when he sold the store.*

After the store was sold Keith and Dorrie took the twins on a lengthy holiday to Southland and it turned out to be a good experience for all of them. Keith had time to recuperate and take better care of himself and Dorrie could finally relax. The twins, who were eleven at the time, seemed a lot better and finally got over the "sickly" label they'd carried through most of their childhood and had good health from then on. When they returned to Blenheim Keith bought a house on Penny Street and was now looking about for some work to keep him busy. Pete, now fifteen and driving, had started working nights at a lucerne factory. He told his boss there that Keith was looking for work and a truck driving job for Keith was soon arranged, which he would keep until 1967.

Pete had also started doing some hay carting and was well into the multi-tasking that would characterise his working career for the rest of his life. And there was more to be added to the local legend of Packhorse Pete:

When I was a teenager, I spent a lot of time working nights and weekends at the old lucerne hay factory with that big rusty silo out on Old Renwick Road. I drove their harvesting trucks, was foreman for a short while and then worked inside on the bagger. There were times when I'd work over forty hours at a stretch between my hay carting work and the lucerne factory at night. My job there was bagging and weighing the hay so you'd have dust everywhere; under your shirt, in your hair, up your nose – it really was a shit job full stop. After you'd bagged the hay, you had to stitch up the bags and then load them into the truck. Now I was quite big and strong for my age and I got extremely fit doing that work and every record at that factory for bagging, packing and whatever I broke. And then I'd break my own records. Unfortunately I used to show off a bit. I don't really like show-offs but I guess my excuse was that I was working there by myself so I was really only showing off to myself though of course word got out to my mates.

The delivery truck at the factory was this old Thames Trader and when I was there alone at night, I'd practise towing the truck with a rope, which I held in my teeth. Don't ask me why – just got bored I guess. So after practising and getting my neck muscles built up, I was able to tow that truck from one end of the factory floor to the other. It was on concrete so it was probably easier to do than it sounds, but others that tried couldn't do it. My mates and the other boys thought this was all pretty good and wasn't Yealands a tough mad bugger towing this truck with his teeth. Well that wasn't good enough for me and after a few months I started loading the truck before I did the towing trick. I just started with a few bags but I kept at it and got to the point where I could tow the truck fully loaded the length of the floor. Yeah I know it was showing off, but it was a challenge.

A few months later an incident at the factory occurred that would strengthen Pete's conviction that he'd really rather be working for himself. He was working alone one night when lucerne dust at the top of the silo caught fire. The rafters in the silo were burning and Pete knew he had a serious problem on his hands. The outside of the silo was made of iron, with a metal ladder spiraling up around it, and he knew he had to get up there fast and put the fire out.

I found the big fire extinguisher and started up the ladder and then about halfway up I realised that I still had my heavy hobnail work boots on. I knew I wouldn't be able to keep my footing once I got to the top as the roof was at very steep angle. So I ran back down the ladder and took off my boots and headed back up again in my sock feet. I finally made it up to the top but by now that roof was bloody hot. I put the fire out but my socks caught fire and I burned my feet pretty badly so it was a tender trip back down the ladder I can tell you.

A little while later, the factory manager, who'd been called, showed up and what does he do but rip the shit out of me! Not a word of thanks for putting the fire out – all he could go on about was that if I'd fallen off and been killed they would've had to shut down and there'd be an investigation and whatnot. And it wasn't my welfare he was concerned about – it was just the consequences it would have on keeping the factory operating. Well I thought stuff it – the next time I'll just let it burn down. I left that job not too long after that.

At the same time, he had also started his first business. Pete and his mate Mickey Swindells had done a fair bit of work together – fencing and crutching – and had always got on well so they decided to go into the hay carting business together. They pooled their slim resources and Pete went out and bought all the machinery, but he'd no sooner bought it all when Mickey decided that it wasn't for him after all. So Peter bought his share out and went on his own. It was hard dirty work and his brother Kevin, who was still in school, would sometimes work for him on weekends.

Pete's first truck was a 1955 Thames Trader 8 ton but he wanted to carry heavier loads so he put bigger tyres on it. It originally had a petrol motor, which he replaced with a diesel, and he put a rack over the top and front of the cab so it could carry an extra twenty-five bales of hay. He could cart 225 bales of hay with that truck, which was a big load and probably too heavy for the vehicle, but he was in business.

I had the truck, a rough-as-guts trailer and a side bale-loader. I remember I charged 8 cents a bale to cart and stack it for any farmer. I was doing that for a while and then Norm McLennan from McLennan's Transport – he had over a dozen trucks, all International trucks with petrol engines if I remember right. Anyway Norm heard about this silly bugger Yealands carting hay on the cheap and he approached me and said he'd give me the contract to cart all of McLennan's hay. To them hay carting was just a nuisance and none of their drivers wanted to do it. So anyway I started carting hay for them and they paid me quite well to start with but then the payments got further and further apart. Then they asked me if I'd cart hay on longer trips like Blenheim to Nelson or wherever. So I in my youth agreed and started doing the longer hauls and all the while they ran up a hell of a bill with me for this. I only ended up getting about half of what was owed to me and I'd been depending on them for most of my income.

But money isn't everything because I'll never forget one trip. I took the first truckload of hay down the Keneperu road, which had just opened, took it down to a chap called Bill Patterson who had an Angus stud down there. He was a good bloke and he had a lovely wife and I remember she was up there helping him unload the hay. Well it was a hot day and she was in a tight t-shirt and sweating like crazy. I always prided myself on getting the job done quickly and getting on to the next one, but I guess I lingered a bit on that job. Funny how that's always stuck in my mind.

A somewhat similar event stuck in his mind when his hay carting took him to Nelson one day. Peter used to visit his auntie who lived on

Toi Toi Street and he had become friends with Margaret Somervail, who lived next door. Margaret was the same age as Pete and they would often spend time (quite innocently by all accounts) in his auntie's back yard. Her house was slightly elevated and overlooked Margaret's back yard, where Peter had noticed a very good-looking young woman. She was quite dark and Peter asked Margaret who the Maori girl was next door. Margaret said there was no Maori girl next door so Pete pointed the girl out to her and Margaret said, "Oh that's my sister, Vai." Peter now had a name to put to the face and when he visited, he could often be spotted craning his neck to see if the lovely girl next door was out in the yard. As it turned out, Vai soon headed off for Australia as she had become involved with an Aussie bloke and no longer graced Margaret's back yard – but Pete never forgot her.

Pete carried on with his hay carting and took on what other work he could find to fill in any spare hours he had. He recalls one time when he realised he didn't have anything to do on Thursday nights so he found a job to fill the space. At the same time, his fascination with machines and vehicles grew and though he was a quick learner and thought he knew quite a bit about vehicles he still had some lessons to learn about engines. When the hay business was quiet, he'd sometimes park his truck for a few days at an engineering shop that belonged to a bloke who did a bit of work for him. Early one morning he went to pick the truck up, jumped in and pressed the starter button but it wouldn't turn over. He tried a few more times, turning the early morning air blue with some salty expressions but still nothing. With a late start for his day's work looming Pete simply assumed it was a flat battery and quickly took action.

I towed the truck to the top of a hill with my car, which was a Sunbeam Talbot and not a big car. I got it to the brow of the hill and had to get it to where I could get some momentum and just as the truck was starting to move, I backed the car up to it to stop it, got out and put a piece of 4x2 timber under the tyre of the truck to hold it there. I took the towrope off, shifted the car, went round to get in the truck and as I got into the truck I kicked the 4x2 out and the truck started to roll down the hill. I got it into gear, let out the clutch and promptly blew a piston out the side of the engine block. As it turned out, the battery wasn't flat at all – it had a piston full of water because the head gasket had cracked and water got in. Pretty embarrassing and it cost a bit to fix, but it never happened again.

Driving in Cars

Never one to fear a change or a challenge, a trait obviously passed on to his children, Keith started a car-wrecking business in Grovetown in the late 60s. He and Pete built a big garage and workshop and Keith soon had a thriving business repairing and selling cars and trucks. Keith had discussed this with the twins and asked that one of them learn a trade and the other one work with him at the garage. They were just out of school at the time so Stephen joined Keith straightaway and Kevin apprenticed himself as a mechanic with the plan to join the business when he got his A-grade mechanics ticket. On his meagre off-hours, Pete started to spend what time he could at his dad's garage watching and learning. Keith had a friend, Doug Robbins, who was a good mechanic and Pete remembers going to the garage at night to watch them tear motors down, fix them and put them back together. He learnt enough that he was soon able to completely rebuild an engine himself, pistons, crankshaft, the whole thing – including, one would hope, being able to recognise a cracked head gasket.

Peter rarely went against his parents' wishes and was generally well-behaved but his independence was starting to assert itself in many ways. He would often ask his dad's advice or Keith would volunteer it when Peter came up with an idea or something he wasn't too sure about. Keith recalls, "I'd tell him I didn't think it was such a good idea, or I'm not sure if that's going to work, and he'd always say, 'I'll show you'. It was just like a red flag in front of a bull if you told him it couldn't be done, and he's pretty much been like that all his life." Keith recalls an incident when they had the wrecking business:

> When Pete was working with me in the garage, I'd often buy a car, we'd do it up and sell it. We'd go over the cars pretty good and get them looking pretty good. We did one for Pete, fixed

it up and he was properly thrilled with it. A little while later, he brought the car over one weekend and said, "Look at this, Dad, come and have a listen." So I went out to have a look and he'd taken the muffler bits out, stuffed the exhaust pipe with wire wool, drilled a hole at the end and put a wire through to hold it there. Of course it sounded very nice, but I told him, "You'll burn out the valves – there's too much back pressure. You'll have to take that stuff out and put the muffler back in." Well Pete wasn't ready to do that and he drove it over to where we bought our petrol and he says, "Come and have a look at this, Sam." Sam comes out, takes a listen and says, "Yeah that's bloody good that is" and of course he was figuring the work he was going to get fixing it. So Pete comes home and says, "I've shown it to Sam Mills and he said it was all right." "Well," I says, "at any rate it's your car – do what you like." And of course it didn't take long till he'd burnt the bloody valves. But that was Pete for you.

A very dangerous incident with long-lasting repercussions occurred in 1965. It started with Pete covetously eyeing a very flash Buick. Keith told him, "Pete you can't afford to run something like that, it'll go through petrol like there's no tomorrow. But there was no telling him different and he got it anyway and he came over to the garage to show it to me and says, 'Well I got it, now what are you going to do about it?' and I says, 'Nothing, Pete, it's your car, your worry.'" A couple of days later he ran out of petrol and Keith, who was still recovering from yet another heart attack, showed him how to pour a bit of petrol down the carburettor to help start it when the tank had been run dry. And he told him to be very careful if that happened again because the petrol will blow back if you put too much in. Keith didn't think anything more about it and Pete drove home.

Anyway a few days later it happened again but I was still crook and he'd got Stephen to help him. Pete got an empty milk bottle and filled it full of petrol and told Stephen to get up on the side of the bonnet, pour the petrol down the carburettor while Pete tried the starter. Well just like I told him, it blew back and it was an awful mess. Stephen had burning petrol all down his front and some on his face and he was very badly burned. He was in hospital for ages and they told us to prepare for the worst – they didn't expect him to live. He pulled through but it left him badly scarred and he grew a beard as soon as he could when he got older, to hide the scars. We all felt terrible about what happened and I know Pete was really upset. Dorrie asked me, "What are going to say to him?" and I said, "Nothing, if I did I'd probably say something I'd regret later. He's learned his lesson." That was definitely the worst thing that ever happened with Pete but I know that mess affected him quite a bit and got him thinking. Pete was his own person and he just wouldn't listen sometimes. Looking back he was a good kid and a bloody hard worker, but sometimes there was just no talking to him.

The garage was an education for young Peter, still in his teens. He would often be over there in his spare time and the big bonus was always having a car. In the teenage pecking order, a car overcomes many things. Think no further than Toad in *American Graffiti* wheeling his mate's '58 Chevy Impala two-tone with the hot blonde in the passenger seat. In 1960s teenage-world, a car could prevail over otherwise insurmountable road blocks on the highway to teen heaven. A car could trump nerdiness, acne, too short, too fat, too anything and Pete was none of these things. He was a strong, smart, good-looking young man, always polite and neatly dressed. He always had a job so he usually had a dollar or two in his pocket and could be counted on to pay his share. He didn't smoke, drank little and he had a car. The only hindrances to Pete's complete conquest of the young women in Blenheim were probably two things: his polite reserve that sometimes bordered on stammering shyness and the fact that he was usually holding down at least two jobs at any one time and was always working – except on Friday nights.

Pete did what most of the young men did in Blenheim. Friday night was the big night in town and Blenheim was a hive of activity for young lads on the prowl. They'd take to the streets on what they called "grummet runs", which was just driving round and round town hoping to entice some girls to come along to a party, of which there were many on a Friday night. He was shy with girls though still managed to have, as he calls it, "a few flings".

> *I tended to hang around with the guys who had more luck with the girls, particularly my mate John Bates. I'd be driving and John would be the one who'd hang out the car window and chat up the girls. After the burnt valves lesson, I'd just loosen up the exhaust pipes on my car to make a bit of noise, though I was never in the running for the hottest car in town. I remember a chap Francis Bray who had a 1939 Chev coupe, lowered with an under slung suspension, leopard skin seat covers, lots of chrome and lights – that was the flashest car in town then. I guess things haven't really changed much.*

He and John Bates had become pretty good mates and in early 1967 Margaret Somervail, Pete's friend from Nelson, shifted to Blenheim. Pete introduced them and John started going out with Margaret. Pete had the idea that Margaret might have been more interested in him but John, as noted earlier, was always quick off the mark with the ladies. And besides, Pete was always busy working. From time to time, he'd think about Margaret's beautiful older sister, but she was in Aussie. That all changed in January 1968.

CHAPTER FOUR

One Thing Leads To Another

With Pete it's always something finishing, something going on
and something new. – **Friend Murray Mears**

It is New Year, 1968 and two things happen at this juncture of the story. Peter becomes a family man, and his story is no longer linear. From this point on, we will see the evolution of Peter's lifelong pattern of having many irons in many fires. Some things will be contiguous to one another, implementing ideas and solutions that have sprouted from the issues and questions of the current task at hand. Others will be completely disparate, springing from a seemingly clairvoyant ability to see what's coming down the road. They will all engage his prolific imagination and his tireless application of hard work.

In 1969 and 1970 he was working at fencing, crutching, hay carting, hay baling and coal haulage. In the early 70s he briefly worked for two companies, he started taking Council tenders for building pathways, cleaning and painting bridges, and his interest and work in the mussel farming industry took shape. He would work at one job during its season, another in the off-season; he would work one job during the day and others at nights and on weekends. Throughout all his work he always maintained an inherent need to see each task through to its logical conclusion. And if that conclusion was to quit or move on to something else, he would do so. He made mistakes and had great successes and through it all he never stopped learning and never stopped working. The reader will see the same date for different jobs, and the terms "at the same time" and "concurrently" will be commonplace – because with Peter Yealands, one thing always leads to another.

Beside Every Good Man

Violet (Vai) Frances Somervail was born in Motueka in 1945 and grew up in Nelson on Toi Toi Street, not far from Tahuna Beach. As she went up through the school system it was apparent early on that Vai was, among other things, a natural artist. She started drawing when she was seven and art has always been an important part of her life. When she left Nelson College for Girls she started working at the Nelson Post Office as a telegram delivery agent. "We delivered telegrams all over Nelson on our push bikes and we joked that our bikes were two-speeds – stop and go. I really enjoyed that job – we worked all weathers and got to know all the short-cuts around town." From there Vai went on to work as an operator at the Nelson toll exchange. Telephone usage had doubled through the 50s and while automatic systems were starting to find their way into the larger exchanges, manually operated boards were still a common-place sight in the smaller communities. The job was important to Vai as her family was very appreciative of the extra income.

Vai's father, James Alexander Somervail, had been heir to a significant brewing fortune by way of his father, Binnie Hamilton Somervail, who owned a "public house" in Hawera on the North Island. When James was four years old, his mother Catherine died in childbirth with her second child and James was brought up by a succession of housekeepers. He was not made to go to school on a regular basis and as such did not receive much of an education. This precluded him from going into the business and when his father died in 1923 the business was sold.

James met and married Vai's mum, Isoline Grace Grooby (née Flowers) in 1940. He adopted Nathalie Grooby, a child from Isoline's previous marriage, and soon there were more children on the way with Charlie, Vai, Margaret and Edward. By all accounts, they were a hard-working family and were well respected by all who knew them.

By the time Eddie was born James was sixty-two and had been doing low-paying work for the local Council. He never owned a vehicle in his life and his hobby was salvaging old bicycles, fixing them up and selling them for extra money. One of the family's main sources of income came from taking in orphans and foster children so there were always lots of kids about the place. The house they owned was on a back section and one of the oldest on the street. The kids all wore hand-me-downs, the foster children included, depending on what size was available. Vai always felt that wearing hand-me-downs was good for her character in that she learned early on to fend off or ignore smart remarks from the other kids at school.

By the mid 1960s Vai had grown into a strikingly beautiful young woman. She was quite dark when she was young and was often assumed to be Maori. When Peter first saw her over the fence, he was pretty sure that she didn't notice this sixteen-year-old checking her out from the safety of his auntie's backyard. And he was right. It wasn't until after Pete and Vai were married that Margaret told Vai about young Pete's interest. He was a fairly regular visitor next door and while Vai was aware of younger kids playing in the next yard, she took no notice of Pete. And even if she had, a three-year age difference between teenagers is just a month or two shy of eternity, and besides she had an Aussie bloke who she was seriously considering marrying. In 1965 she left her job at the Nelson telephone exchange and headed off across the ditch to Brisbane to pursue the relationship.

Brisbane was an education for the young woman from small-town New Zealand. She had hoped to pick up a telephone operator's job there but her inability to wrap her tongue around the Aboriginal place names in Australia put paid to that and she ended up working as a nurse's aide. She recalled without resentment one amusing incident when she was at the hairdresser's and a girl there commented on what a pretty Aborigine she was. Old hat to Vai; same comment, different tribe. However, the relationship with her Aussie fellow was not working out and after two years in Brisbane, enough was enough and she returned home in 1967.

In the meantime her sister Margaret had shifted to Blenheim, where she was working. Vai wasn't too keen on staying in Nelson so she joined Margaret and they shared a flat in town. Vai needed a job and Margaret was working at, as Vai called it, a "knicker-factory" – lingerie manufacturer actually – on George Street and was able to get Vai work there. Vai recalls, "I wasn't very good at it, at least not in their eyes, because I was too meticulous. You could wear what I'd sewed inside out but of course they were more interested in speed and quantity so that job didn't really work out." But Vai was soon to have more than reversible knickers to occupy her mind.

In early January 1968 Margaret, who was dating Pete's mate John Bates, suggested she and Vai go to a dance out in Grovetown that Saturday night. Peter still had the idea that Margaret might be interested in him – after all they were the same age and had known each other for quite a while. He thought that Margaret had brought Vai along to keep John busy while she made her move and Vai corroborates this notion. At any rate, the two girls walked the mile or so out to Grovetown but when they got to the dance, the boys had already left. They stayed for a while and then headed back into town. But Margaret was not easily discouraged.

She talked to John early the next morning and suggested that he take her and Vai out to Robin Hood Bay. It's a postcard-perfect little bay with a good beach a few kilometres north of Rarangi, about a half-hour drive out of Blenheim, and was a regular spot for a day at the beach. Margaret was pretty sure everyone – including Pete – would be there and sure enough they were and there was lots going on. Some were camped up on the beach, others out in a dinghy fishing and diving for paua and everyone was generally carrying on the way teenagers do at the beach. Confirming Peter's suspicions, Margaret had earlier asked Vai to make sure she got in the front seat with John on the way back, but Vai was a little piqued at her sister's suggestion. She thought Margaret should take care of her own business and not get her involved and besides she was not really looking for a boyfriend. Vai was just looking forward to a nice day at the beach.

When Pete saw Vai he must have thought back to those surreptitious peeks over the fence at Nelson and now here she was tagging along with his mate's girlfriend – and looking very good. If Margaret had any ulterior motives they were now dead in the water – Pete only had eyes for Vai. As Vai tells it, they got talking and she and Peter seemed to hit it off straightaway and felt quite comfortable with each other. She didn't think he was shy, just a bit more reserved than the other boys and this suited her fine. As Pete tells it, he passed on Margaret's advances and ended up in the back seat with Vai when they all headed back to town. Margaret had managed to keep her dodgy intentions hidden from John and the four of them ended up going to the movies in town that night. Pete knew he was on to something special and wasted no time. Three months later they were engaged and in August they were married.

By all accounts it was something of a whirlwind courtship. Vai remembers that Peter was always working and didn't have much time for the usual teenage antics. While Vai was a big Elvis fan, Peter never paid much attention to music and remembers that if you asked him what that song was on the radio, he wouldn't have a clue. Visits were made to Nelson and introductions to Vai's parents and vice versa in Blenheim. With Vai living in Blenheim now she got to know the rest of the family and Pete's dad Keith recalls one incident in particular. "I remember one night Pete came home in the wee hours and I saw two figures slink down to the river bank and I think they had a pretty heavy session going. The next day I said, 'Better be careful there, Pete, you don't want to get anyone up the duff or anything like that,' and he says, 'Don't worry about it, Dad, I know when to stop,' and I laughed and said, 'Well then you're a better man than ever I was.'" It was one of the very few times Keith offered some advice and Peter didn't say, "I'll show you".

The only dark cloud for them during this time was the health of Vai's father. He was in his mid seventies now and not well. But one weekend he decided he wanted to visit Vai and Margaret so he grabbed his pushbike and headed off for Blenheim. Those who live in the area will know that between Nelson and Blenheim is the northern end of the Bryant Range and the only way through is SH6, running through the various saddles down to Rai Valley, where the road then levels out through Havelock to Blenheim. James was struggling to get to the top of the Whangamoa Saddle, just 30km out of Nelson and 600m up, but it was too much and he soon got off the bike and started walking it up the hill. A TNL truck driver saw this old chap walking slowly up the hill and stopped to offer him a lift. When they got into town, the truckie asked where to drop him off but James didn't know where the two girls lived. He told the driver a bit about Pete, who was still driving for McLennan's at the time. The truckie was a local chap and figured out who James was talking about and took him out to Keith's home in Grovetown. So James had his visit and Pete and Vai drove him and his bike back to Nelson.

On 3 August 1968 Peter and Vai were married at the Church of the

Nativity in Blenheim. Pete had just turned twenty and Vai was twenty-three. They didn't have much money – Peter remembers that when they got married they had the grand sum of $100, which had to cover their two rings and the wedding party for over a hundred guests. Vai contributed with her dress-making skills and designed and made her wedding gown and the gowns for the bridesmaids. They were a good-looking young couple and Peter remembers that it was a very special day and everyone had a wonderful time. The Yealands family was well known and respected in Blenheim and it was common knowledge that Pete was a hard worker and would always provide for his family.

A Family Man

For their honeymoon Peter had hired a caravan and with that in tow behind his Sunbeam, they took off for a two-week trip to Southland and back. Their first home together was a rented farmhouse at Fairhall, just a few kilometres west of Blenheim. The little house was stuck in the middle of a small farm and the owner gave them a good deal on the rent in return for tidying the place up. The property allowed them to keep a varied menagerie of ducks, chooks and a few goats, sheep and calves. At the time they got married, Pete was still driving for McLennan's but a week or two after they moved into the Fairhall house, Pete brought bad news home one day and said the job was over. The only thing he really knew much about then was hay and he decided to take it to the next level and start his own hay-baling business. He'd done a bit of hay carting for a chap who lived in Grovetown who had since opened an agency to sell farm machinery.

So of course he said to me, "What you need, Pete, is a baler" and he sold me this bloody great big Freeman baler – I was an easy sell that's for sure. I bought it on a hire-purchase and it wasn't cheap – probably somewhere around fifteen grand or so which was a lot of money then. It was big and fast but it made the bales quite a bit bigger than was usual in the area, so I figured that would be my trademark – "Big Bales from Big Pete" – or something like that. So here I had this great big flash baler but I couldn't afford a decent

*tractor so I had this old clapped-out Massey Harris 101. It was a
weird-looking thing with a Chrysler flat-head 6-cylinder petrol
engine and only had three working gears and one road gear. They
dated back to the middle of the war and if you were lucky it could
get up to 20mph in the road gear. But it worked and that first year
I actually did extremely well and picked up a lot of new clients plus
those that I'd carted hay for. That was when I first got to know
Peter Radich. He'd just started his law career and helped me chase
up a few outstanding bills that were owed to me.*

The second year, though, saw a bad drought in Marlborough and it
almost finished Pete's new company then and there. Hay was very hard
to come by so Pete came up with a plan to put molasses into barley straw
bales. Barley straw was at the bottom of the stock food chain and the
whole idea was to make it palatable to the stock.

*I came up with the idea when I remembered some farmers asking me
to put salt down on the bales when I was stacking it because the stock
liked the flavour and I figured molasses would taste better than salt.
Each bale had about 10 slices in it so I built a pressure pot, filled
it with molasses and rigged it up on the baler so that each time the
baler did a slice, it would inject molasses into it. I picked up a bit of
business and all I charged was 2 cents a bale extra with the molasses
but in general everyone was too miserable to pay the extra 2 cents.
It was too bad actually because it worked very well and the stock
liked it, but to no avail. I ended up storing a lot of it and I can still
remember the wonderful smell of those bales on a hot day.*

At the same time, Peter had also become interested in a correspondence course put out by an organisation called the Australian
Correspondence School. The course covered all forms of construction,
building, concrete block laying and quantity surveying and estimating.
What he didn't realise at the time was that the course had no validation
in New Zealand and that much of the content was quite outdated. Peter
flew through the course but then found that the qualifications were of no

official use. As disappointing as that was, the learning provided him with a solid background in many aspects of construction and this combined with his constant willingness to get stuck in to hard work proved to be of considerable value.

He had also started to look into the fledgling mussel farming industry. There were considerable tax benefits to be had and Peter started writing letters and reading up on the subject. Vai recalls, "Back when we were first married, Peter had already started thinking about the mussel farming and did a bit of research on it and decided to give it a go. And I can remember when he told his family about it, they all said he was absolutely bloody mad and got a good laugh out of it. Of course it didn't take long for them see that firstly he was quite serious about it, and secondly it was a pretty good idea and of course they soon joined up with him and away they went."

But full-time work in the mussel industry was still a few years away and in the meantime he kept at the hay baling and also added coal carting to his CV.

In the off season, I'd buy up all the straw and hay I could find and stick them in a shed on some land I'd leased from the railways. I had thousands of bales stored in there for quite a few years and sold hay all round the top of the South Island. In the winter, I used to cart coal as just about everything back then ran on coal – probably 2000 tonnes a week coming into Blenheim from the West Coast. So I stuck a hoist on my old Thames Trader and I'd take hay down to farmers on the West Coast. Once that was delivered and paid for, I'd nosy around for cheap coal at the mines, which I'd pay with the cash that I'd just got from the hay sales. It wasn't bagged, all bulk sales, so when I got back to Blenheim I'd bag it up – very often at night time if I was busy, which I usually was – into 50–60kg sacks. I had some good customers, a lot of pensioners I remember, and it was all done on a cash basis. I'd bought an old '37 Chev that I cut the back off and put a deck on it and that's what I'd use to deliver the coal around town.

Anyway the following year there was another drought, which pretty much finished my hay baling business. I ended up taking the baler back to the dealer and said, "Look, I've paid half this off so you can have it and we'll call it square." He agreed to it so in the end I walked away with nothing. They were good days though. I used to do a fair bit of work for some farmers up the Waihopai valley and here I'd be coming home at three or four in the morning with this old Massey Harris flat out, spewing sparks out of the exhaust and making an awful racket.

And now it wasn't just Pete and Vai – son Aaron was born in June 1969 and daughter Danielle would follow in August 1972. The birth of his children affected Peter and his choice of work while the kids were young and for a while he put his entrepreneurial inclinations on the back-burner. After the hay baling died out and knowing that he had more than just himself to worry about, he hired on with T.H. Barnes & Co. in Blenheim. The family had also outgrown the little farmhouse in Fairhall and moved to a rented house on Howick Street in Blenheim. They didn't stay long there as they wanted to purchase their own home and soon a property came on the market that they thought they could manage. At father Keith's urging after he left school, Peter had got into the habit of putting half his pay into the local building society. They used his building society shares and took on a small mortgage and bought a house on Fell St (now Lansdowne) in Blenheim for $7500. It was the first house they owned and they also became neighbours of solicitor and life-long friend and colleague, Peter Radich.

T.H. Barnes & Co. was and still is a thriving construction company in Blenheim. In 1970 Pete signed on as a rigger and was soon at work driving the piles for the new ferry terminal overpass in Picton. The Wellington to Picton ferry was now an integral part of New Zealand's rail and road transport system and the infrastructure to handle the ferries in Picton was a major construction project at the time. There were severe site constraints as this was all being built on reclaimed land on what had been not much more than tidal swamp and mudflats on the Picton foreshore. It was big-time civil engineering and Pete was a hard worker and avid student at the site. It was a whole new experience and from this he picked up considerable bridge-building experience that he would later make use of.

Pete was always looking for things to scavenge and the site manager at Picton had tipped him off about a concrete shed that was available. It was not overly big but weighed close on 25 tonnes due to the concrete walls, floor and roof. Pete reckoned he could lift it with a crane onto a transporter and shift it back to Blenheim and use it for a shed in the backyard of the Fell St house. It being on the construction site, there was no shortage of cranes and step one was completed, hoisting the heavy shed onto a transporter. When he got it home, he rang Musgrove's in Blenheim to hire a crane and crew to get it sited on his property. The problems began when he found out that Musgrove's largest available crane was only rated for 20 tonnes, so Pete hedged a bit on the details and told them yeah, that should work. Musgrove's came out to the house, set up the crane and began to lift the shed from the transporter and hoist it over the fence and into Peter's back yard. They got it off the transporter, over the fence to some extent and partly down, but then the laws of physics took over and the crane tipped over. The shed dropped to the ground undamaged but on a very weird angle and several feet away from where Pete had set out a foundation. The crane crew were soundly ticked off and had to go get another crane to lift the first crane back up. This done, they told Pete to get stuffed and left the shed where it had plonked down in his backyard.

And now Peter had a problem. He'd already dug out a foundation so with crowbar in hand went round the misplaced shed and inserted sticks of trusty gelignite into the surrounding mud and dirt around the shed. He had used gelly before on fencing jobs and reckoned he knew what he was doing. He did some rough calculations on how much force was needed and where so there would be one stick here, two sticks there, some deep, some shallow. He then packed it all down with lots of mud to get a good compacted explosion and wound up with sixteen charges planted and ready to go. The whole idea was to lift the shed up from where it was, push it over a few feet to the foundation and drop it down into place – at least that was the plan.

So I set this thing off and it was a massive bloody bang. The explosion shredded all the washing that Vai had put out on our

*clothesline, splattered mud far and wide including the washing in
Peter Radich's backyard. It was an awful mess. But when the smoke
cleared and the mud settled, the shed had lifted up, moved over
and settled perfectly onto its foundation, where it sits to this day. I
couldn't believe it and looking back it was definitely a fluke, but it
was also great fun. A quarter of an hour later, there were police cars
all over the neighbourhood trying to find out where this huge explosion had come from, but they never found me.*

While Peter was working for Barnes in Picton at the ferry terminal, another construction company, Fissenden's, had the contract to do
the surrounding earth and stone seawall for the new terminal. The whole
building site had been constructed on reclaimed land and would require a
sturdy seawall to protect it all from water erosion. The seawall was to be
made from tonnes of rock and boulders that had already been transported
to the site but as they were primarily earthwork and bulldozer operators,
Fissenden's had little interest in doing this final stage of the work. As it
turned out, no one else was interested either and they couldn't find anyone
that would take on the work. It was not a machine-friendly job and would
mostly entail brutally hard manual labour moving tonnes of rock into the
required positions. They had even approached some local rugby clubs to
come down and do it on weekends, but still no takers.

Peter heard about this and realised that Fissenden's were in a bit of a
bind. He managed to get a very sharp price for the job and got his brother
Kevin, who was engaged to be married, and a few other mates on board
for the job. He put them all on contract and they worked like navvies evenings and weekends getting the seawall built and everyone, particularly
Peter, made a small fortune. Kevin made as much in the six weeks it took
to complete the work as he would usually earn in a year and it gave him a
good start to his marriage. The work was very tough going, manhandling
rocks and boulders, some half a tonne or more, and the only equipment
they had was an old borrowed loader with no brakes which they dunked
several times. But they got on with it and the work went so well that Peter
secured more stonework around the terminal itself and went on to make
a lot of money from the project. He was still earning wages from Barnes

at the time so this work was all done evenings and weekends and would set a precedent for his later mussel venture. The money, as Peter says, "put me on my feet" and was really the start of his business endeavours. He had seen what the combination of hard work, ingenuity and the brass and balls to take on a big job could financially accomplish and it would set the pattern for much of his work in the future.

When the Picton work was done, Peter moved on and did a stint with Glenroy Products in Blenheim and rapidly became a foreman with a sizeable crew working for him. At the time Glenroy were fabricating large industrial cooling and refrigeration units and after a short while working in the factory learning and building, they put Peter in charge of their outside contracting work. The position involved a lot of travelling around the South Island and Peter managed a big chiller installation at a large meat-packing plant at Pareora, south of Timaru.

> I went down with six staff to do the work and I remember that when I left Aaron was just starting to talk. I'd be down there for three or four weeks at a time and then on one of the times I was away, Aaron stopped talking. I guess me being away must have affected Aaron to the point where he missed his dad and it has stuck in my mind ever since – made me think a bit too I can tell you. At any rate, my work down south was going really well and we picked up lots of extra work and I took on an even bigger staff. When I got back after the job was done, I approached the management at Glenroy and pointed out that I'd been doing much more work than I had signed on for and was hoping for a rise in my hourly rate. But they told me I was earning more than they were what with all the hours I was working which were something like 90–100 hours a week and they had to say no. So after less than a year with them, I left and never worked for wages again in my life.

Working for Pete

Running concurrently with all his work in the early 70s was the infant mussel farming industry. He was past the reading and asking questions stage and was becoming ever more committed to giving it a serious go.

He had also interested father Keith and brothers Kevin and Stephen and all four of them soon found their evenings and weekends very busy. But, as will be discussed in the next chapter, the industry was barely on its feet and it would be some years yet before it would return a decent profit, so they all kept working and attended to the mussels in their spare time.

In 1972, Peter started doing a lot of work for the Marlborough County Council, taking on contract construction work building footpaths and sewer lines, building, cleaning and painting bridges.

Whatever came up in tender, I'd usually take a shot at it. I remember the bloke who handled all the council contracts. He was a tough nut but he loved his whisky and the story was that provided he got his whisky, you got your contract. Well I always made sure that he got his whisky but I think he looked a little deeper than what people gave him credit for, because even with the whisky I didn't always get the contract, but I got most of them.

Brother Kevin would often help him with contracting work. "He was a hard worker and did well. He worked fast, quality work; just got on with it and didn't let things get in the way. I think for Peter sometimes it was easier to seek forgiveness than permission, but he was always like that, even when we were kids."

At this time, Pete and Murray Mears became good friends and Murray still works for Peter managing his Blenheim vineyards. Peter picked up a job painting the roofs of all five buildings at RNZAF Base Woodbourne and Murray was assigned to help with it. However, after a day's work, Murray had to beg off because he was uncomfortable working on heights. Pete had no issue with that and finished the job himself. They carried on working together and did a lot of bridge work, sand and water blasting and painting. Pete reckons they did every bridge in the Awatere Valley and some of son Aaron's early memories are tagging along on those jobs. Pete also did bridges for the railways on the West Coast and jobs for the Ministry of Works.

He still had his trusty Thames Trader and he'd also purchased four old Land Rovers from the Government Stores Board in Christchurch.

He sold two of them and kept two. One of them he converted and put "a bloody great big" water blaster on it, installed a power take-off hooked up to the gearbox and used it for all his bridge work. He'd put a pump on it and would drive down to a creek or river, fill the water tank up and then take it to the job site. It would be a big job to do each bridge: sandblasting to get all the grime and whatever off, water blasting to clean everything up and then several coats of paint. Getting underneath was a problem and Pete designed and built an under-slung harness apparatus that would attach under each span of the bridge and would give them a decent platform to work from. Whether it would pass current OSH standards is not known, but it's more than likely it would. Peter might have had a healthy touch of Heath Robinson in his mechanical imagination but he always took the well-being of himself and his crew quite seriously.

But it wasn't full-time work on a regular basis and even though Pete would answer any and all tenders that came up they could be months or even years apart. This gave him the opportunity to unleash his entrepreneurial side and try all sorts of things. It's hard to believe now but he tried rabbit farming. He built a long run at the Grovetown property and actually made a good dollar at it until the market went away. Possums were tried as well but as Murray says, "They were a mess to work with – we ended up killing and skinning most of them."

He and Murray formed a company called Frosty Fish and net-fished for kahawai on the Wairau and exported the product to Australia. The business was quite successful, though they did get into a bit of bother from time to time. They found early on that it wasn't just kahawai that got caught up in the netting – there would often be lots of very nice trout as well. The boys figured they might as well make the best of it and would smuggle the trout out and sell them on the quiet to local restaurants. They were done in not by skeletons in the closet but by skeletons in the back alleys behind the restaurants and wound up getting nicked, although usually resulting, as Murray remembers, in nothing more than "a slap on the wrist". Pete and Murray also built a very large metal box net, several metres square, which they dropped into the Wairau River. It was very effective but Harbour Master Don Jamieson caught wind of this contraption sitting in the Wairau and had a word with the boys, telling them it just wasn't on and to remove it.

Frosty Fish was well into its second successful year and Pete found that he needed more product. He hired more people to fish for him but when a "possie" battle broke out, with the fishermen getting up earlier and earlier to get the best position to fish, they were soon right down to the mouth of the Wairau and the fish never had a chance to get up river.

It has been a long, strong friendship between the two of them and Murray has been there working with Peter from the early days, through the mussel farming years, Kaiuma and now the vineyards. It wasn't all work, says Murray:

> We got up to quite a bit of mischief in those days. We both loved hunting, especially pigs, and just about every weekend if we weren't working we were up in the Sounds pig hunting. One time in Southeast Bay in the Sounds, Peter chased a bloody huge pig – over 200lb when we finally weighed it – and the dogs got to it down the bottom of a very steep hill. Pete went scrambling down to stick it and slipped and fell all the way down the hill and landed with a bump right in front of the pig, which grabbed Peter's foot in its mouth and would not let go. Pete couldn't go up – too steep – couldn't go down – the pig. I was laughing like a fool but Pete was in a bit of a panic by the time I got down. "Stick that bloody pig – it's not funny you know," he was yelling, but I tell you it was pretty funny and he laughed after we finally stuck it. Then of course we had to haul this bloody big thing back up the hill, but Pete just slung it over his shoulders and clambered back up the hill.

Long before jogging was trendy, Pete and Murray used to run round the Waterlea Racecourse to keep fit. One weekend they had nothing particular to do after their run so they thought they'd go out to the Adams property on the North Bank of the Wairau and shoot some feral goats they'd seen out there on a job.

We parked Pete's old Triumph Herald on the road and went up the hill and sure enough we found lots of goats. We had a good time up there – shot lots of goats – but then we got a surprise. We thought they were feral but when we got up close after we'd shot them, we found that they were all tagged. Well, what are you going to do now – can't take the bullets back so we dressed them and started back towards the car. It was towards evening and we were coming down the hill and saw a bunch of people and lots of cars around our car and we thought "oh shit" and sure enough the Adams mob had heard all the shooting going on up the hill and were standing by the car waiting for us. "What are we going to do?" I says, and Pete says, "Let's just wait for a while." So we waited for a while but then the cops showed up. "Crikey, Pete, we're nicked – now what?" But Pete was pretty cool and he says, "Stuff it, let's hide the goats and our guns, wait till dark, and then we'll sneak across the pad-docks, and then just walk up the main road and pick up the car and go." We waited till dark and we're in the paddocks but now some of the Adams boys had their motorbikes out and they're haring around looking for us. One of the young boys was head-ing towards us on his bike and when his headlights hit us full on he got the fright of his life, screamed and slid off his bike. Anyway we got to the car and saw everyone and we said, "So what's going on?" – but they knew it was us. The cops went up later on and found some shells, got our rifles and matched them and all that. Anyway, we ended up getting done for that – $100 each. The Adams mob were known around the area for being a bit scratchy so the court went pretty easy on us – the judge says, "Pay your fine, boys, and don't do it again."

In 1974 during a conversation with brother Kevin, who was look-ing to buy a house at the time, Peter said why not buy their house on Fell Street. Peter had already acquired a sizeable section in Grovetown where he planned to build a house. Kevin was renting a house on Penny St from father Keith so they agreed to a deal and the two families swapped locations. By 1976 Pete owned the Penny St house, put it on the market and purchased a large caravan. It was time to shift to Grovetown and in late 1977 they moved into the caravan, where they would live for close on two years while Peter was building the house in his off-hours.

As usual he didn't think small and put together plans for a Mediterranean-style villa that would provide close to 500sq metres of floor space. He designed the house himself and sourced the bulk of his material from his contacts for his Council work. With the exception of the tiled roof Peter completed most of the work on his own with the help of any mates he could persuade to lend a hand. The house was built in Pete's spare time – he was still working and by that time he was very busy with the mussel business – but Vai remembers those days well and apart from the cramped quarters in the caravan, it was a good time for the family. The kids, now eight (Aaron) and five (Danielle), thought this was all quite exciting – it was one big camping trip for them – and Aaron recalls thinking that perhaps one day this house would be his. And then there was the swimming pool.

Pete included plans for a swimming pool in the project. Murray was always around at the time and he recalls vividly its somewhat improvised construction.

I helped Pete with building the big stone house in Grovetown. When we got around to doing the pool, the weather turned bad and someone went out for beer and Pete, me and a few other blokes ended up having a contest to see who could get the biggest load in a single bucket scoop with the digger. It seemed that as the beer went down the scoops got bigger and bigger. Each of us would dig out a scoop and dump it and we'd all take a careful look at the size of the mound and that's how we'd keep score, but after a few scoops were piled up we forgot whose pile was whose. So now we'd all have to have another go and this went on for quite a while, or at least until the beer ran out, and somehow the pool ended up a lot bigger than originally planned.

Bigger indeed and when the boys were done it was the largest pool in Marlborough. The exaggerated size also meant that it would need a lot of chlorine to keep it clean so Peter came up with a sophisticated filtration system that would not require constant and expensive doses of chlorine.

It involved a serious amount of baking soda and an even larger amount of salt and the idea was that the water gets softened by the baking soda and partially turned into brine from the salt. The salty water was then pumped through a machine that produced chlorine as the water went through it. The treatment part was essentially a big electrical element that caused a chemical reaction, which produced the chlorine. The system actually worked quite well and the powder and salt were cheaper than chlorine so I was pretty happy with it.

But one night when Vai and I were sleeping we were woken up by just a massive explosion. I got up and went out to investigate and saw smoke coming from the pool filter shed that housed the chlorinating system. The roof was blown off and everything inside was destroyed. When the mess was later analysed it became apparent that through a mechanical or electrical fault, the system had not shut down automatically and vast amounts of chlorine were being produced which eventually exploded. I decided not to rebuild the system and regular chlorine additive was used from then on. Too bad really – it was a pretty good system.

Aside from the exploding filter, the house was a great success and became the centre of Peter's activities for the next eighteen years. Pete could be close to his work and still see the family regularly and watch the kids grow up. Vai was taking care of the kids and was also keeping involved with her art and painting. She'd had a few lessons, but mainly taught herself. She branched out from drawing to work with pastels, acrylics, pencil and charcoal, silk screening and Chinese brush painting. And although she considers herself "a hobby artist", she's had several exhibitions over the years with other like-minded artists. The house was also the focal point for socialising and Murray recalls that "we had a lot of great times out at that house – Christmas, holidays, and weekends and the like. Peter used to take more time off back then for that sort of thing – doesn't seem to have that sort of time these days, but we sure had some good times."

Keith's practice of buying in bulk had rubbed off on Peter and he became, as he calls it, "a bit of a trader". He was always on the lookout for a good deal – usually in bulk – and one of his favourite sources was the Government Stores Board (GSB). The GSB would put out a catalogue every month or so covering goods from all of the government departments. From the Post Office, the Defence, the railways, printing works and anything in between, there would always be a huge variety of goods that the government needed to get rid of. They would call tenders for the surplus goods and they rarely had a bottom line or reserve on the price. Pete would go through the catalogue and put a bid on every second or third item, with bids as low as $10 on things that might have originally been worth thousands. And if no one else put a bid on it he'd win it – and he won a lot. He'd buy pretty much anything: bulldozers, engines, supplies by the trainload including six train car-loads of paint at one time. He recalls that he always had a colossal amount of stuff around that he'd bid on and of course he had to get rid of most of it.

Daughter Danielle recalls one result of all this surplus buying:

There were always banged-up old cars and trucks around the place – Bedfords and the like, rarely nice cars like everyone else had. And that wouldn't have been too bad except that around the same time, Dad had got this deal on drums and drums of post-office red paint. So everything – cars, trucks, walls, sheds – just everything was painted in this deep post-office red. When I got dropped off at school or when Dad picked me up from somewhere, it seemed that whatever he was driving was post-office red. Looking back it's quite funny but it wasn't that funny when you're a kid and your friends are having a go at you about it. But that was just Dad being Dad.

One of the really interesting buys Peter made was when the Navy tendered their torpedo filling station at Devonport. The station was made up of several good-sized rooms filled with some very arcane equipment that had been used in the war and later to fill torpedoes. At the time, the Navy had two people looking after all this equipment, which amounted to little more than cleaning and polishing, so they wanted it gone. So Pete bought the lot (excluding torpedoes) for what he recalls was about two or three thousand dollars. The prize item for Peter was a huge Gardner 803 diesel motor plus a room full of spare parts for it. All the gear took up several rail wagons to transport from Devonport and when it duly arrived in Blenheim Pete started selling off the separate bits. Just selling the brass and copper pipe paid back his initial investment. There was a massive air compressor that he sold for a good price to a diving company who used it for filling air bottles and now he was into profit on his purchase. He eventually sold the diesel to a chap in the Twizel area who had a big earthworks business, although Pete thinks that the motor ended up in a very flash boat the fellow owned. But before he sold the diesel, Pete just had to have a go at it.

*This diesel had an air starter – no electric starter – and had origi-
nally been started from the compressed air in the torpedo tubes. I
knew it was air-start but I was determined to fire it up at least once
before I sold it. I had the motor up on mounts in my driveway at the
Grovetown house. The motor had a huge flywheel of maybe four feet
in diameter with a hole in it. I put a bolt in the hole, tied a nylon
rope around the bolt and wrapped it round the flywheel and tied the
other end to the front of my Land Rover. When all was in readi-
ness, I'd drive in reverse as hard as I could to try and start this huge
motor. Well this bloody thing just wouldn't start, and I knew my
way around diesels but I just couldn't figure it out. I tried and tried
but nothing and I finally gave up on the idea. But a few nights
later I had an inspiration that perhaps I was going the wrong way.
I'd been pulling it the way a conventional motor turned but maybe
this was different. So the next day I went out, hooked it up the other
way and on the first compression this massive motor roared into
life. It then dawned on me that many twin engine boats have each
engine rotating in opposite directions to reduce vibration and such. I*

*took a good lesson from that – don't take anything for granted which
way an engine runs. But that was a bloody marvellous motor I can
tell you. Would've loved to have kept it but I had no real use for it
and it did fetch a nice price.*

The early 70s in New Zealand were a time of great change. In 1971
both the Tiwai Point aluminium smelter and the Warkworth satellite
station began operation and a year later the Values Party, considered
the world's first national-level environmentalist party, was established at
Victoria University in Wellington. Also in 1972 the Equal Pay Act was
passed and on 25 November a Labour Government led by Norman Kirk
was elected. In 1973 New Zealand's population reached three million,
colour TV was introduced and a year later the Commonwealth Games
were held in Christchurch. In 1975 Lynne Cox became the first woman to
swim across Cook Strait and on 29 November Robert Muldoon became
Prime Minister.

In music, young Tim Finn in Te Awamutu was putting together
a band called Split Enz and Kiri Te Kanawa was gaining international
stardom in the world of opera. Kiwis were reading Dick Scott's *Ask the
Mountain: The Story of Parihaka* and Barry Crump's *Bastards I Have Met*.
In 1974, historian Michael King's six-part *Tangata Whenua* was the first
in-depth examination of Maori culture on television. In 1972 another
great All Black team, led by Ian Kirkpatrick, Sid Going and Alex Wylie,
again went undefeated through the home unions, marred only by a 10–10
draw with Ireland.

The population of Blenheim had grown to over 17,000 by 1976
and throughout this period Peter Yealands had been finding his feet both
in family and work. He had taken on the responsibility of providing for
Vai, Aaron and Danielle. He had seen what could be accomplished with
imagination and hard work. He had also seen instances when his way of
doing things could rub others up the wrong way. But Peter knew that over
the long haul the job would always get done and to him that was the most
important thing. And the job now at hand was mussels.

What had started as an embryonic idea in 1969 was growing to full
maturity and by the middle of the decade Peter's focus was firmly on the

fledgling industry. It would prove a turbulent but ultimately very reward-
ing endeavour. It would bring him closer together with his father and
brothers and then bitterly split them apart for many years. It would tax
Peter's ingenuity and innovative spirit to the maximum and, as always, it
would lead to other things.

CHAPTER FIVE

Making the Waves

It won't be long before mussels are a big industry, if we are allowed to get on with it.

Before we look at Peter and his part in mussel farming in Marlborough, here is a brief primer of the New Zealand mussel farming industry, with thanks to the New Zealand Marine Farming Association and Marlborough Online. There is also an excellent in-depth history of the industry written by Carol Dawber entitled *Lines in the Water*[2] upon which I've drawn for this chapter.

Mussels 101

The native green-lipped mussel (*Perna canaliculus*) farming industry was established in the early 1970s, and since then the mussel aquaculture industry has grown phenomenally. Mussels are now New Zealand's second most valuable seafood export, generating from \$175–\$200 million a year. There are approximately 645 mussel farms in New Zealand at the time of writing. The average lease is 3–5ha, although farms may vary from one hectare to twenty or more. Farmers do not own their farms but are granted a licence to use the water space. Each 3ha farm will typically have nine longlines of 110 metres each. Each longline will support 3500 to 4000 metres of crop line. Each longline is supported by 50 to 70 polypropylene floats, each of which can support one tonne.

Mussels were harvested by hand from intertidal rocks until the 1960s, when a dredge industry attempted to satisfy local demand. Mussel beds

2. Dawber, Carol, *Lines in the Water*, River Press, Dunedin, 2004.

in Tasman Bay and the Hauraki Gulf were quickly dredged out and a few people turned their attention to mussel culture. The native green-lipped mussel was used to trial a cultivation technique in which young mussels (mussel spat) were grown on ropes suspended from rafts. The sheltered, clean waters of the Marlborough Sounds, rich in nutritious plankton, provided an ideal environment. After a year to a year and a half the cultured mussels were ready for harvest and the first went on sale in 1971.

As more growers entered the industry, the labour-intensive raft method of cultivation was dropped in favour of a modified Japanese longline system. Biodegradable stockings (mussock) full of spat are tied to parallel rows of looped ropes supported by buoys. The young mussels grow through the stockings and anchor themselves to the ropes with threads formed by a special secretion. For some years ropes were reseeded after harvest with spat found growing naturally in local coastal waters but the timing and volume of supply was unpredictable. In 1975 a marine scientist discovered abundant mussel spat attached to washed-up seaweed on Ninety Mile Beach in Northland. Local people began to collect the seaweed, pack it into buckets and air freight it to mussel farmers. Kaitaia spat has become the main source of seed mussels in New Zealand.

During the 1970s mussels had been exported to the United States as a powdered health supplement to relieve arthritis symptoms. This market collapsed overnight in 1981 when stringent drug legislation controls were placed on the powder by the US Food and Drug Administration (FDA). Subsequently extracts from mussels were developed in New Zealand, where they continue to be marketed as health products.

By the mid-1980s fresh green-lipped mussels were cheap and plentiful in New Zealand supermarkets and the industry turned its attention to developing reliable export markets. Frozen mussels in half shells became the dominant export item, patented with the trade name New Zealand Greenshell™ Mussels. By 2000 the industry was booming: mussels were New Zealand's second most important seafood export, with sales of $170 million to over 60 countries.

There it is – a world-class product and industry started by a few tough-as-nails pioneers who combined vision, innovation, persistence and back-breaking labour. On 10 November 1975, coincidentally the thirtieth wedding anniversary of Keith and Dorrie Yealands, an article appeared in the *Marlborough Express* reporting that:

> The first marine farming licence for the Sounds has been issued by the Ministry of Agriculture and Fisheries (MAF). The licence is for a one-acre area in Ruakaka Bay, Queen Charlotte Sound, and is issued to N.Z. Marine Culture Co. and is for a 14-year term. A director of the company, Mr. P. Yealands of Blenheim, said four rafts were already in position in the bay. The delay in granting leases or licences has worried local authorities, particularly the Harbour Board which permitted rafts to be moored at its pleasure in anticipation of an overall policy and planning by the ministry. The first licence was applied for in 1969.

New Zealand Marine Culture Co. comprised Peter, Keith and Peter's brothers Kevin and Stephen. The issuance of the licence was the culmination of years of bureaucratic bumbling and procrastination on the part of the Ministry of Agriculture and Fisheries and the Ministry of Marine versus the dogged determination of the Yealands and a few other early farmers. It wouldn't have happened without the unwavering support of local authorities, who combined selective rule-bending with a benign blind eye to allow the pioneers to get started. It wouldn't have happened without the support of the academic community, who provided expertise in the form of committed marine biologists. And it wouldn't have happened without the likes of the Yealands family, who thought that mussel farming sounded like a pretty good idea. It was – and here's how it happened.

Early days

In 1968 much was made of the new Marine Farming Bill that passed through its second and third readings in Parliament in December of that year. The bill contained forty clauses and set out the legalities of applying for a lease and the handling of applications and was much touted at the time. In hindsight and in actual implementation, the 1968 bill proved to be an unworkable mess to administer and its only real benefit was to highlight the need for something better. Its main flaw was that it was based on leases, which required the Marine Division to sign away rights to the entire seabed, rather than licences to use the area. That single issue accompanied with frustrating governmental vacillation and fear of setting precedence proved its undoing. It was a start and if nothing else at least brought the issues to the fore, but as Carol Dawber accurately summarised:

> The Parliamentary select committee was under no illusions about the workability of that marine farming bill. It was based on mussel farming patterns and practices in Spain, Japan and America, and everyone involved knew that there would be totally different conditions, constraints and challenges in getting a New Zealand industry up and running. *Those who entered the industry would be heavily reliant on their own experiences and resources, but the potential was boundless.*[3]

A seminal meeting was held in Wellington in October 1971 and was attended by politicians, scientists and the marine farmers. What everyone wanted to get their hands on, especially the farmers, was the document covering the new Marine Farming Act 1971, which had passed through parliament the previous month. It was hoped that this new legislation would redress the problems incurred with the 1968 bill. It addressed the key issue of leasing versus licensing, and reverted to a licence that provided for a more restricted and qualified permit. The new Act gave MAF the responsibility of issuing licences and also gave much more consideration to navigation and property rights. It also set out detailed requirements for rafts and other structures to be well-constructed, safely moored, well-marked and lit and deemed it an offence to interfere with the work of a licensed marine farmer. Everyone in attendance left the meeting with positive feelings about the progress made and anticipated

---

3. Dawber, ibid.

the timely issuance of all outstanding licence applications. But it was not to be: foot dragging and red tape continued to bedevil the process. The farmers couldn't wait and decided to get on with it as best they could.

From a practical standpoint, the methodology at the time was based on the Spanish industry, which used rafts. Experiments had been tried in the Hauraki Gulf with rafts that had bunches of ti tree branches suspended beneath them with the hope of catching spat, which would attach to the brush and grow. Various types of rope were tried, as the ti tree bundles tended to fall apart in heavy weather, and a reliable spat source had yet to be found either in the Hauraki Gulf or in the Marlborough Sounds. There was a lot to learn.

A Family Together

Peter had been curious about marine farming as early as 1968. His interest had been initiated by some very advantageous tax benefits that the government had made available to encourage the industry: full agricultural tax write-offs on capital expenditures instead of depreciation, plus 20 per cent accelerated depreciation allowance and 20 per cent investment allowance would be available to those interested. In 1969, Pete's hay-baling business was in its first year, he had made some decent money and was now faced with the issue of paying taxes. These benefits made a lot of sense and Peter made some enquiries and wrote some letters to find out more.

He was the first in the family to get stuck into the business and for many months worked on his own in his off-time. He was quite busy then with his contracting work for the Council but he was keen to get the family involved and saw it as an opportunity for them to work together. This was very important to Peter as he had been on his own pretty much since he left school. When he got the job to build Keith's wrecking business garage he had enjoyed working and being with the family. He was very positive and persuasive about this new industry and soon had worked out a partnership agreement with his dad and brothers.

I'd been working on this on my own for the first six or seven months
– all evenings and weekends – and then my brothers and Dad

got involved and we put a company together called New Zealand
Marine Culture. The original shareholding was that I had 7/8 of the
shares and my brothers and Dad had one share between them. So if
I put in $7000, they put in $1000 or $333 each. After maybe a year,
I started feeling the pinch money-wise as we were putting in a lot of
money in equipment and the pressure came on to me to sell them more
shares. I was still working at other things, bridges, footpaths and the
like and I almost feel as if I was forced to because I had a hell of a lot
of other things on the go at the time. At any rate we agreed to each
of them having one full share each. So whenever we needed a capital
contribution, I'd put in $5000 and they'd put in $1000 each.

As to the equipment needed, Peter had contacted Bert Batenberg,
one of the very early people in the business who was more of a mechanical engineer than a marine man and he was trying very hard to get the
structures right.

Bert was very encouraging to start with but he was really hung
up on the engineering side of things and I guess he was a bit of
a perfectionist as well. Anyway, our lot got stuck into building
ferro-concrete rafts and had a raft in the water while Bert was still
thinking and designing. But he was very important at the start,
especially for his enthusiasm. He had a real way with words and
had Henk Hilhorst, a reporter at the Marlborough Express, very
interested and Henk provided a lot of positive coverage over those
early years. But I just wanted to get on with it and after a while
Bert and I drifted apart.

Of great assistance at the time was the support from local regula-
tory bodies, especially Marlborough Harbour Master Don Jamieson and
Bob Pennington and Dave Olliver at the Marlborough County Council
(MCC). Don Jamieson recalls:

A real issue was the difference between MAF and the Marlborough Harbour Board both controlling the same water but with

MAF having precedence. We started approving farming structures as moorings. MAF knew it, but didn't make too much of a fuss and probably were happy with the idea. Then the Marlborough Sounds Maritime Parks board was formed at that time and they controlled the land and reserves and obviously took interest in what was going on in the water in front of their reserves. So the Harbour Board, Park Board and the County formed a small advisory group and drew up plans defining where they would object to marine farming. The farmers then asked that instead of a negative plan, how about drawing up a plan to define where they *could* go, which they did. Jim Jenkins then got involved and set up the standard marine farming space of 3 hectares.

Myself and the Harbour Board were very supportive of marine farmers. First we had the 1968 Act, but nothing happened because it was based on the issuance of leases as opposed to licences and it was just unworkable. Even after it changed in 1971 it still seemed to take an awfully long time to get to the stage of issuing licences. Bruce Hearn and Peter were real players, but soon the word got out about the potential of the industry and we had the "Queen Street farmers" getting involved and we had to eventually place a moratorium on everything until MAF got their act together. Victoria University was also very supportive and interested and had experimental rafts in Shakespeare Bay at the same time.

That first batch of rafts was a pretty poor lot – 44 gallon oil drums and that sort of thing. Peter was not alone doing things by seat of the pants – getting in and doing it and asking afterwards sort of thing. Even the first longlines were on oil drums until the plastic floats were developed and Peter was the first one to manufacture them in large quantities.

Bob Pennington, County Manager, and Dave Olliver, Deputy County Manager, were also closely involved with and very supportive of the early farmers. Says Dave:

Prior to the RMA in 1991, the jurisdiction was pretty loose –
Council, Harbour Board, MAF – and nothing was really nailed
down as to who determined what could happen in the water. I
know that there was no frustration or delays with local regula-
tory bodies but there was a lot of frustration with MAF over
the delay in issuing of licences. Where we did have definite
jurisdiction was land-based processing facilities and we had
no problems getting them going. But the frustration of marine
farmers has always been there, and it still is present. Then it
was lack of decision-making, now it's the dual process due to
the RMA.

Another issue to local bodies was the positive effect that the industry
would have on the area itself. Bob Pennington explains:

In 1970 there was deep concern about the depopulation of the
rural areas. Rural school rolls were dropping and rates as well.
Council knew that marine farming would bring people back
to living in the Sounds. The MCC was very supportive of this
and the marine farming turned this around and more people
moved back to the Sounds. As to dealing with the farmers
themselves, there was very little conflict among them – not
like today where there might be disputes over territory. Not
that the Yealands weren't protective over any new tricks they'd
learned – they tended to keep them covered up for a while but
word usually got around that someone had found a better way
of doing things.

Dave adds that while Peter could be hard to negotiate with "once
settled his word was his bond".

His reputation for butting heads with authority might have
become somewhat inflated over the years. Once we had
something sorted, we never had any major problems with Peter.
There were a lot of grey areas back then and Peter and the

family weren't too averse to taking advantage somewhat but they were probably no different from lots of others back then who just wanted to get on with the job. There certainly was a lot more discretion back then – both for us and for them. The RMA has tightened everything up which over the long run is obviously a good thing but it's not a stretch to think that much of what those early farmers did pre-RMA could not be done now. But my hat's off to Peter – he has been a true innovator, always improving techniques and equipment and as hard-working as they come.

Jim Jenkins, a tall, lanky American who obtained his marine biology degree at the University of Washington in Seattle, came to New Zealand in 1972 to work for the Fishing Industry Board as a marine aquaculture biologist. He would become a leading figure in the young industry and for those who were there at the coalface he was and is considered to be one of the most important shapers of the nuts and bolts of the industry. He was a scientist, but also a hands-on guy and was able to apply his highly specialised skills and knowledge to practical and workable methodology for the Marlborough marine farmers. Jim recalls,

We were the Jacques Cousteau generation and there was huge enthusiasm where I went to school for fisheries and there was this great exchange of information and a network of keen people. There was a lot of talk at that time in the 60s but action was minimal in the States. I finally got really fed up with the whole situation and backpacked down to New Zealand in January 1972 and fell in love with the country and the people. I spoke with the New Zealand fishery people and found a lot of common interests and when I officially emigrated, I had one interview with the Fisheries Industry Board and started right away. And I can remember on my first day on the job in late 1972, there was a letter from Peter Yealands on my desk. Their farm at Ruakaka Bay in the Sounds was already on the go and Pete was still waiting for their licence.

In the early 70s, the biggest concern was know-how. There was now widespread interest and MAF was sitting on a considerable number of applications. In 1972 a public meeting was held in Havelock to form an organisation called the Marlborough Sounds Marine Farming Association. It was hoped that their pooling of efforts and knowledge would hasten the development and give those early farmers a chance to talk and compare. Its first president was Bert Batenburg and Peter was the first secretary. He stayed on with the committee through 1974 but then left and neither he nor anyone else in the family took further part in any of the industry associations. In the meantime, Jim Jenkins was hard at work putting prototype farm plans together and lobbying hard in Wellington to free up the bureaucratic quagmire that was still holding back the issuance of licences.

With the whole family now involved, the Yealands' first job was the fabrication of rafts. With nothing to guide them, they decided to build them from ferro-cement.

We decided ferro-cement was the way to go and we built a big concrete wall with metal outriggers so we could laminate large beams up out of 6x2 radiata glued with epoxy and clamped together. The beams were 25m by 50cm and the pontoons were lined with the 6x2, coated with netting and then glued. We ended up with four pontoons, two each for two rafts and they turned out pretty good. We slung them up on the transporter and unfortunately one of them cracked on the way, but we got one in and it was the first raft in the Queen Charlotte Sound.

The next thing we needed was spat and we decided to try and catch our own. We asked Don Jamieson at the Harbour Board for permission to put spat rafts in the water at Shakespeare Bay. This was well before the big logging port that's there now, but there was a freezing works there and a lot of algae in the water. The spat rafts were pretty rudimentary, mostly a bunch of 44 gallon drums lashed together, but for the purpose they were okay and we hung rope from them and caught a fair bit of spat.

From there the spat was taken over to the big rafts in Ruakaka Bay and they were in business. The mussels grew quite large and consequently quite heavy as well. At this point they ran into the biggest conundrum of the early farming. They had permission to build rafts, install them as moorings, catch spat and hang it on their rafts and grow the mussels. What they still didn't have permission to do was actually harvest the mussels. The family's frustrations were reaching boiling point and Peter got hold of the *Marlborough Express* to publicise their concerns. It must be remembered that at this time the licences were expected to arrive "in the near future". The new 1971 Act had supposedly paved the way for a virtual rubber-stamping of the outstanding applications and the farmers were under the impression that the licences would be shortly forthcoming.

And so the Yealands waited. The paperwork piled higher and higher, the mussels grew heavier and heavier, the rafts sank lower and lower until the freeboard was minimal. Mother Nature, or Murphy – take your pick – then got into the act with a large storm and the rafts sank.

We were absolutely gutted and looking back we should have stripped them I guess, but there was so much effort and money involved that that just wasn't on. We got permission to put in another raft to salvage what we could and went down and raised them by putting drums in the hatches. In the end we ended up losing half the mussels but at least we got the rafts floating again and actually ended up with 70 tonnes of mussels that year.

Another thing that came out of that mess was that both we and the Harbour Board reckoned that we should probably find a better place. Where we were in the inner Queen Charlotte Sound was quite busy and somewhat restricted so we made application for a licence for Mills Bay in the Keneperu and moved everything over there. We'd have more space, more privacy and decent spat had been found there as well.

At the same time, they got away from the ferro-cement and started making polystyrene and fibreglass rafts. They would put a coating of latex paint to form a layer between the polystyrene and fibreglass and then blocks of polystyrene were glued together with plywood and covered with fibre glass. They had almost a production line on these. They could build one a week in the shop that Peter had built for Keith, truck them out to Havelock and put them together in a few hours right by the boat-loading ramp and into the water. They could hang anywhere from 200 to 400 ropes off them and could move the ropes around to different places on the raft. They then made a steel mould that was more streamlined, which meant they could put them together without painting them first. They made dozens and sold quite a few and Pete thinks there are still some of them floating around.

By this time I was putting a lot more time into the mussels during the week and my brothers and Dad were still working at the wreckers and working the mussels on the weekends. I took a crack at building a boat and sold it to the company but it was a bit of a disaster – too small, too short and had a crapped-out motor in it. The next one was better.

The next one was indeed better. If there was one thing they'd found out it was that fully grown mussels in the quantity they were harvesting were very heavy. Any working boats would need both space and grunt and so Peter built the 32ft *Venus*, based on a Pelin hull design, and it was a huge improvement. Known for its excellent rough water-handling characteristics and a deep-V hull that planed easily when empty, the design was a good choice for a working boat in the Sounds. But even then they'd occasionally overload it and the consequences could be painful and embarrassing – as they found out one day when they were bringing the *Venus* back to Havelock with over 150 bags of mussels on board.

We were coming in to Havelock one day with Venus very heavily loaded when the electric bilge pump failed and we didn't notice it until we saw all the water slopping around. We were frantically shifting the mussels around and restacking them so we could get into the hold and put in the spare bilge pump. But that only went for a few minutes and failed too. As it turned out, both the bilge pumps were labeled 24volt but were actually 12volt.

We definitely weren't going to dump the mussels overboard and we didn't even think to put them off on the beach so we carried on in, bucketing flat out. We started having problems at Keneperu Head, got to Cullens Point and the boat was starting to rock and tip and as it rocked we'd all run to the other side to right it.

We knew we were in the shit and we kept heading for the wharf hoping we could get there and tie up before it tipped, but there were too many boats on the wharf and we had to tie on the outside. As we got there we all rushed to one side but it was too late, it tipped and went straight to the bottom beside the Havelock jetty – what a lot of mud on our faces. We got the fire brigade down, pumped her out enough to lift her and had her up and floating in no time but we lost the mussels. My brother went down the next day and salvaged them all and scored the money.

Another issue to be faced was friction from the established fishing people. Now that they were running out of Havelock, there would be more contact with the fishermen who had been working Pelorus Sound for generations.

A lot of people took the mickey I can tell you. I remember we were up to our waists in water assembling a raft one Saturday in Havelock and there was Bruce McManaway on the Tanekaha *with a bunch of blokes having beers and slinging off at us about trying to farm mussels when dredged ones were there for the taking. It wasn't long afterwards that he was farming them too.*

And many fishermen were naturally opposed to rafts of any kind in the water. Further scrutiny came about when a storm broke up a heavily-built concrete pipe raft in Fairy Bay, leaving a large concrete pipe standing up like an oil rig. The Ministry of Transport was very concerned, for obvious reasons, and it was decided that mussel rafts would have to pass survey.

When we found out that the rafts would have to pass survey, we modified our design to the approved length and size and rebuilt our steel mould to make the new pontoons. That was easy to sort, not like the crap we were getting from MAF, who were still pissing about with the licences.

I remember one summer, must have been November 1974 and we were refused permission to harvest our mussels in Mills Bay because the law then made no distinction between wild mussels and farmed mussels and the "official" season had finished at the end of October. We were told we should try to change our farming schedules to make sure we'd harvest in the right season. That's the sort of attitude we were always up against – nobody in Wellington wanted to make a decision and we were out there working like navvies trying to make a go of it.

Mussels, as it turned out, were easy – spat was the big issue. Finding it, catching it and keeping it. The Yealands and Jim Jenkins had some success finding and catching spat in Shakespeare Bay but it was not a consistent source and they got thinking about building their own hatchery. They built a hatchery at Rarangi, where they were immediately besieged by complaints from the locals and disclaimers from scientists, saying they had nothing to do with this private venture. There were further objections when an intake pipe broke and by the end of 1974 the hatchery had still not produced spat. The Yealands and the other farmers carried on with what they could find naturally and then in August 1975 a discovery that would change the Marlborough mussel industry was made on Ninety Mile Beach in Northland.

Two fisheries officers were taking routine samples along the beach and came upon massive clumps of stranded seaweed that were completely covered with mussel spat. After analysing the samples and verifying that they were indeed *Perna canaliculus* – green-lipped mussels – they sent some down to the Yealands, who immediately established some on their lines, and to Jim Jenkins, who started studying and testing it. From that point on, it became a cottage industry in Northland collecting spat, which was then flown down to the Sounds and used by most of the mussel farmers.

So now that they had spat, the next issue was keeping it.

*Another big problem we all ran into was spat predation. I think it
was the same year and we had a marvellous spat crop, but when we
pulled the ropes up to check on them we found less spat on them every
time. We set a gill net off the beach and caught heaps of big fish, all
sorts of variety and when we gutted them we found they were full
of green mussel spat. We thought about that during the week and
we came back the next weekend we found 95 per cent of our mussels
were gone. It was devastating.*

Larry Collins, who worked for Peter through the 70s and 80s,
remembers one of the spat predation solutions. Blokes being blokes, they
reckoned that there weren't too many problems that couldn't be sorted
with a few sticks of gelignite.

We'd get plastic shopping bags and fill them with stones and
half a stick of gelly and drop them into the water around the
spat rafts. And it worked quite well and a few days later Pete
said he was going to take the little dinghy across the bay to
do some other spat rafts he had. Murray Mears and I stayed
working where we were and could hear these dull booms across
the water and then Pete comes back and this bloody boat was
absolutely chocka with snapper and there's Pete sitting in the
middle of it up to his knees. So he said we'd better stop working and get all this fish filleted, so that was quite a nice bonus.
That method almost backfired on us one day when we chucked
a bag of rocks and gelly overboard and the bottom of the bag
broke and all the stones fell out leaving the bag with the gelly
still on the surface and floating back towards us. We were running around like hell trying to get the boat untied and Murray
finally did get us away before the gelly went up. But MAF soon
got onto our gelly business and told us we had to stop because
other mussel farmers had started doing it too. We reckoned we
were only protecting our crop, but I guess we did push it a bit.

Peter tried hanging nets over the side of the spat rafts but they'd end up getting clogged and stopping the circulation around the spat that was needed for healthy growth. Then he had a go with rotenone, which is the active ingredient in Derris dust and is used as a fish poison in some of the Pacific Islands. Peter acquired the rotenone in powder form and reckoned that the best bet would be to form it into pellets that could then be dropped into the water around the rafts. The only problem was that Pete didn't have a "rotenone pellet-making machine" so, ever the DIY bloke, he figured out a way to process the powder by using Vai's electric mixer in their kitchen. Pete mixed up the rotenone with salmon food and fish oil in what he thought were the right proportions but during the process he started breathing the fumes of the rotenone and almost passed out on the floor.

Yeah, I got woozy mixing it up – you have to be careful with that stuff. And actually it worked quite well on spotties and didn't hurt the mussels at all, but there was a huge uproar and the Marine Farming Association thought the publicity was really bad for the image of the industry and we stopped making it.

The spat predation would be a constant problem and perhaps it's why mussel farmers were sometimes seen fishing off their spat rafts during smoko – it was just another form of spat protection and the bonus was those very tasty Sounds snapper.

Longlines

Though the rafts had pretty much graduated from the bulky and potentially dangerous concrete rafts to the lighter and more manageable polystyrene rafts the Yealands were building, rafts still had serious limitations. Cried one newspaper headline, "How would you like to see your boat run into a moving object which is capable of sinking the Queen Mary?" The new rafts were smaller but they would ride high when empty and couldn't be adjusted or have extra buoyancy added when the weight of growing mussels pulled them down. They were large and not cheap and required a substantial capital investment to get started. There was also a problem of food getting to the mussels on the inside ropes. Something better was needed and the advent of longlines would revolutionise the industry. It would also pave the way for Peter to branch out from farming and become fully involved in the design and manufacture of equipment to the industry.

The pivotal person in the switch to longlines was Jim Jenkins, who remembered the longline systems he had seen for oyster culture in Japan. "They were small neat structures, so individual people could play around with them. I started wondering why they wouldn't work for mussels. I was also sure if a boat-load of people drowned after hitting a raft, we would have no aquaculture future. I went back to Japan to study marine farming in 1974 and when I got back I got onto Jim Campbell [FIB general manager] to import 50 oyster floats."

The floats duly arrived and were quickly approved by the Harbour Board and the Marlborough Sounds Maritime Park Board. The floats also caught the eye of Federated Farmers, who had always hoped that land farmers in the Sounds would eventually extend their farming into the water. They and others saw the floats and longline system as a way for anyone to start small and build up by adding a few more floats.

Keith Yealands recalls, "Jim Jenkins came back from Japan really keen on the longline idea and after we'd had a look at his floats we built a longline in Mills Bay from 44 gallon drums with chain links welded on. But the first rough sea saw drums all round the Keneperu – it was a disaster." While they admitted that they'd been a bit hasty using steel drums and not floats and that they hadn't allowed for the tolerances needed to keep the chains from breaking, Keith remained working with the rafts. However, once the floats were clearly established as the way to go, the next problem was sourcing them. Importing from Japan was fiscally out of the question and there were no local sources. Peter saw the future and it was building floats.

The Licence

All the while, the battle with red tape continued. The new 1971 legislation had not achieved what was expected and licence applications were still languishing at MAF. Word was out about the great potential of mussel farming and they were besieged with a flurry of applications and, as Don

Jamieson noted, not all from local farmers. The market potential was now spurring speculative applications – the aforementioned "Queen Street farmers" – and MAF was still unable or unwilling to expedite the process. It came to a head in 1973 when the Harbour Board had no recourse but to place a moratorium on licence applications until the mess was sorted out. While local bodies were trying to accommodate the farmers and keep the practical issues in order, MAF was retaliating by blaming them for the delay. Finally in November 1975, the first licences were issued: Number 1 to the Yealands family and Number 2 to Bruce Hearn.

As always the *Marlborough Express* was vigilant in exposing the struggles the farmers were enduring due to Wellington red tape. Many stories and headlines would follow, some quite ironic considering the problems with licensing and several of these articles can be found in the appendix. The following article in the *Marlborough Express* on 22 May 1976 epitomised the frustration with the licencing process.

> [...]PROBLEMS LISTED
>
> Mr Paul Currie of the Ministry of Agriculture and Fisheries listed the problems to be sorted out before an application became a licence. These were numerous and ranged from water purity, cadastral precision of the sea surface, from seaworthiness to indemnity.
>
> Mr Currie said he had received 69 applications for mussel farming. He expected 18 licences to be offered to the applicants by the end of June. If they could comply with the conditions, mainly for exact survey, their licences would be issued. The 18 were for the applicants who had spatlines out. The procedure for a licence had two stages, he said – a statutory period of four months to allow objections, followed by seven to eight months at least "for technical and administrative reasons".
>
> Mr Currie said it was "essential" that the area be precisely surveyed. This could take months and could cost the appli-cant $600 to $700. An environmental impact report could be required and this could take two years.
>
> Mr Rowling [M.P. for Tasman] wanted to know why it still

took six weeks to offer licences to the 18 applicants who had spatlines and stood to lose them. Mr Currie said the minister had not yet decided on the objections.

Mr Rowling also wanted to know why it should take two years to decide on an environmental impact report. That, said Mr Currie, was a matter of policy which he could not explain to the meeting but would give to Mr Rowling in private if he wished.

It would still be a few more months before the Yealands received their Mills Bay licence. Peter's recollection of Currie is succinct: "A bloody dipstick, and just too scared to set a precedent."

A Family Apart

The licence battle had finally sorted itself out and over several years the farmers had brought the industry to a point where returns were starting to be seen. As noted the Yealands' was the biggest operation in the Sounds, but the licensing frustrations had left their scars and had exacerbated an already tense atmosphere within the Yealands family business. As more time, effort and capital was sunk into the business, the pressure mounted on Peter to relinquish more of his holdings in New Zealand Marine Culture to the others. The capital injections required were also a burden on Pete and in 1976 they worked out a new share structure that saw him retain 40 per cent and Keith, Kevin and Stephen now having 20 per cent each. But Peter now found himself in a position he had vowed to never be in again: working for somebody else. And as far as Peter is concerned that's when the partnership with them stopped working.

It started falling to bits with rows, disagreements and at the same time my other work was suffering and I couldn't get a worthwhile income out of them while I was working on the mussels. This was when I reckoned I should pull back from the actual farming and stay on as a silent partner but my participation in the family company just wasn't working. I approached the others and asked them to buy me out and failing that I'd sell my share to someone else. They had in the meantime formed another company – Marlborough Mussel Company (MMC) – but continued using the assets of the first company – boats, vehicles – and I felt I was getting milked and had had enough. The relationship had already deteriorated to the point where there was no question of me joining their new company MMC. They agreed overnight to buy my shares and the money really helped out at the time. Looking back, it was just typical bloody family nonsense.

And with that, Peter was no longer involved with the family mussel business. The split was probably the best for everyone, but relations with his father and brothers were strained for some time. Keith, Kevin and Stephen carried on with MMC, turning it into a major company that was eventually sold in the 90s to Pacifica for over $25 million. Keith would be awarded an OBE for his contribution to the industry.

Peter was thirty years old, with a young family, but he was not finished with the mussels. He had formed his own company, Industrial Marine 1973 Ltd, and he would go into manufacturing the equipment needed for the growing industry. As usual, he was front and centre with ideas and implementation and Industrial Marine would become a very successful and profitable company.

Throughout the 80s Peter would again become directly involved with mussel farming. He would also form a timber exporting company, build seawalls, buy and rebuild boats, wallow in and get burned by the share market craze, farm deer and plant forests. Peter Yealands was just getting going.

CHAPTER SIX

Riding the Waves

Pete could do the whole package and he was local. – **Friend Chris Godsiff**

B y the late 70s, Peter had detached himself from the family business. He was busy at home, still building the Grovetown house, and he and Murray Mears had formed Frosty Fish and were making a decent go of kahawai fishing and exporting. Peter was still taking on any contracting tenders that came his way, but as usual this was all going on at the same time and his main focus was on mussel floats and the company he had formed earlier, Industrial Marine 1973 Ltd. Mussel farming was now going to longlines and floats were replacing rafts. The Yealands had stayed with rafts for longer than most as they'd put a lot of money and effort into them and had a lot of them in the water, but Peter knew that floats were what everyone would be going to. After the bad experience they'd had making their own floats from 44 gallon drums, it was clear that plastic was the best alternative.

With no local supply and the Japanese floats too expensive Peter decided to make his own and the first step was to get a mould. He went to a local engineering company in Blenheim and was pretty excited about it and asked if they could design and build a mould for him. They said yes they could but nothing happened for a long while. This went on for months with Pete pestering them and then finally he went over there one day and there was a mould that they had built using his idea.

I was pretty pissed about that so I figured the only thing was for me to build it myself. It must have taken me days of intricate welding and I finally got a mould made. I had done a bit of research and found out that to make the floats you need a gyroscopic rotational moulding machine – whatever that was – but once I was able to figure out what it did, I reckoned I could make it do what it was supposed to do. It was really not much more than heating plastic in a mould and then spinning the mould. I started with a Triumph Herald car differential to spin the mould – I used the Triumph diff because I had one – but the ratios were all wrong and it promptly fell to bits. So after a couple of months of trying various things out, I ended up using a Mark IV Zephyr differential, which worked pretty well.

The other big problem was heat. When you have melted plastic spinning around inside the mould in an oven, the plastic could cook up on you and you'd have an awful mess trying to clean it up and get it going again. Well I didn't have much money back then and I needed a warning system of some sort. Now I'm a great believer in the no. 8 wire philosophy and in this case I actually used some no. 8 wire. I ran a length of it from the oven to the machine, attached it to a plastic string which was tied to an old baked-bean tin full of gravel. And if the thing got too hot, the heat came along the wire, melted the plastic string and the tin of gravel would drop onto the ground. And it actually worked and about once a month or so it would go off and you could hear this tin of gravel hit the ground.

Peter found a ready market for his floats and as business increased he was able to refine the manufacturing process, though the original moulding machine would remain. He was able to install a more sophisticated heat control system and as always was looking at how to improve the products. He was also adding mussel spat stocking – mussock – and anchors to his inventory and could source other equipment such as lights, ropes and netting as needed.

Chris Godsiff was another member of the early group of New Zealand mussel farmers. He and his family were long-time residents of the Marlborough Sounds and Chris spent most of his early working life in the fishing business. He had worked up and down the West Coast fishing crayfish and tuna and in 1976 was attracted to the mussel farming industry that had just started in the Sounds. Mussel farming had by this time moved from rafts to longlines and floats and anchors were the two main commodities they needed. Godsiff's supplies initially came from Kinnears and Donaghys but their needs were such that it made more sense to buy locally if they could. When Peter talked to Chris about supplying their company, Chris recalls that Peter was "pretty sharp" and they soon came to an agreement. Peter was prepared to work on a cost/plus basis and he was making floats and anchors and had access to a lot of other equipment. He also impressed Chris with his innovation and inventiveness. It being a new industry, a lot of the equipment needed didn't exist and Peter was always coming up with new ideas and better ways of getting the job done.

> Pete could do the whole package and he was local so it worked out very well. And his ability to think up new ideas and solve problems was really something. If we took a problem to Pete about a piece of equipment or just needed something that didn't exist, we'd talk it over and a few hours or days later you'd get a phone call from Pete, sometimes in the middle of the night, and Pete would say, "I've sorted it, this is what you've got to do" or "This is what I've made, and I tell you what, I'll make one and you go try it out, and if you like it I'll make some more" so you really couldn't ask for more from a supplier. He would spend hours working out problems and my goodness he was clever. Some of the things he came up with were pretty wild but they always worked.
>
> One of his really practical ideas was a very useful design addition on his floats that saved us huge amounts of time. The big problem with those early floats was that it was very difficult to lash the ropes to the float backbones and Peter came up with this lug and spanner arrangement that was bloody marvellous. With this setup we could rig twenty floats in the time it used to take to do one and he made that part of his regular float design. He was always inventing things to make the job simpler and quicker because he'd been out there himself and knew how

important your time was.

Sometimes you'd call him and say we couldn't get in to Blenheim to pick up some gear we'd ordered and he'd say, "Don't worry, I'll put it on a truck tonight and get it on a boat out to you in the morning." That sort of thing really sticks in your mind and no one else was offering that kind of service. Pete was a very special businessman and would go the extra mile when others didn't. He was on the ground here in Blenheim, had the infrastructure and the marine know-how. And when times were tough or you were waiting for the mussels to be harvested, Peter was very lenient and would say, "Take the gear and we'll worry about it later," and that was very much appreciated I can tell you.

It was this service and expertise that were attracting more and more customers to Industrial Marine, including Marlborough Mussel Co. Keith Yealands had made it clear to the boys that they would be buying their supplies from Peter. Dealings between them had thawed considerably since Peter had left the first company and Peter was glad to have their custom and their friendship again. Larry Collins was now working for Peter on a full-time basis and the business was spreading out and enlarging behind Pete's Grovetown house.

I was making thousands of floats and going through a 20ft container of plastic powder a week and was one of the biggest importers of plastic into the country at the time. It turned out to be really successful business for me – a good month I was taking in two or three hundred grand and this was all out of my back yard behind the Grovetown house. It was a bit of a rabbit warren out there – a garage with bits added on as I needed them. Looking back, it's hard to believe that over ten years that little home-made contraption that couldn't have cost more than $200 to build went on to make over 200,000 floats and bring in over $13 million in revenue.

Peter and Murray Mears had also set up an equal partnership

company called Anakoha Mussel Farms, which was put together for the development of marine farms. Through Anakoha, they had applied for a licence to farm scallops at Okaha. The idea was to catch scallop spat in the Sounds and put it directly on to the seabed at Okaha and later carefully harvest them without destroying the bed. The concept was new to MAF and not surprisingly they weren't too sure about it. The local fishermen's association wasn't keen on it either and Pete fought and fought for that. They had also applied to have four mussel licences around the edge of the bay, but the whole of the middle of the bay was where they were going to do their scallop farming.

> *MAF said, "Look, it's bloody hard to prove that the scallops you're farming are from the spat you put in. When normal wild spat settles, how can you tell the difference?" And they thought they had us on that but we had an accredited marine scientist from Nelson who wrote us a letter and said that there was a difference because when you put the cultured spat in, it leaves a tell-tale ring on the shell. Here was a biologist supporting us and MAF had a bit of egg on their face after that.*
>
> *In the end MAF gave us all of the mussel licences around the perimeter at Okaha and pretty much told me, "Look, Peter, we're giving you these mussel licences but forget the scallop thing." In the end I think we ended up with around twenty-five mussel licences or so. At the time the licences weren't all that valuable – $200 or $300 – but we knew they would be one day and we ended up selling quite a few of those licences for ten grand each.*

In the early 80s, Peter got back into mussel farming with a group of Wellington business people. Anakoha along with Ray Jurie at Wairau Fisheries joined eight Wellington business people and formed Pelorus Aquaculture Ltd, which was one of the first companies to be made up under the new Special Partnerships Legislation. The format is advantageous where there are a large number of participants in a high-risk venture that is capital intensive and where one or more general partners tend to have particular expertise. It was a natural fit for this type of venture – Pete,

Murray and Ray provided the expertise and the Wellington partners put in the money.

Peter did well out of this. He was a partner in the company and was also supplying it through Industrial Marine and he remembers laying over 200 mussel lines for Pelorus Aquaculture. The partnership carried on successfully until 1987, when Wairau Fisheries sold off its assets. One of the investors in that Special Partnership was Malcolm Brown, a senior broker and financial advisor in Wellington. During this partnership, Malcolm got Peter interested in the share market, which was soon to be deregulated.

Industrial Marine was not limited to marine work. Peter was still contracting to the Council for bridge work and other tenders that came up and would take on whatever he could fit into his increasingly busy schedule. But as his marine business increased, he wanted to expand his ability to both farm and to contract to other farmers for the placing of lines and anchors. For that he needed a large boat and in 1982 he found an old scow for sale in Wellington.

The Success

Peter purchased the scow *Success* in early 1982 from Barney Daniels in Wellington, who'd had the contract for collecting and removing all the rubbish from the foreign ships in Wellington harbour. The boat was 70ft long, with a 20ft beam and a 3ft draft. It was built in the North Island in 1925 and carried an English registry – an impressive document. Pete remembers it was wrapped in cotton cloth, with a portrait of Queen Mary and included a full log-book recording all owners and major events in its history. The scow was the last of its type to be built in New Zealand and had originally been used for shipping silica sand from Ninety Mile Beach down to the glassworks further south. As can be imagined it was in a somewhat distressed and filthy state when Peter took possession and it almost foundered on the trip back across the Cook Strait to Picton. The scow was put into survey and it took almost a year, and a good chunk of Peter's money, before it would be ready for work.

In the early days of the mussel farming, I'd already dealt with

Bernard Foley, who was the official surveyor in Picton at the time, and though Foley really loved what I was doing he still came down pretty hard on me. He was a lovely bloke but was very tough, which looking back was obviously in everyone's interest. I had a lot of help from a chap, John Jenner, who was an English shipwright and he really knew his way around the job. We had to take out close on twenty-five tonnes of old Kauri timber which had rotted and Bernard made me put new timber in, which wasn't cheap then. We pretty much had it down to a skeleton of keel and ribs and redid just about all the wood on the boat.

It all had to be done in the traditional way — bevelling and corking the timbers, tallow between the sheathing on the outside — and it had these big old marine bolts that dated from the twenties. The bottom had originally been sheathed in totara to keep the worm out and much of that needed replacing but we used marine-treated pine instead. The total refit cost over $75,000, so along with the $25,000 purchase price I had quite a lot tied up in the boat. That boat was a lovely thing when it was finished, and gave me good service until I sold it to Rob Pooley in 1990.

Along with all the structural timber work, Peter also replaced the original two 1944 72hp 4L3 Gardner diesels with 6-cylinder 6LXB motors, which were lighter, more powerful and much newer. The 6LXB displaced 10.45L and at 1500rpm the engine developed 127hp. Peter also installed a hydraulic crane and built a spacious wheelhouse with forward-angled windows over the original engine room. Manoeuvrability was going to be a key issue so Pete designed and built bow-thrusters made from Hamilton jet units driven by hydraulic motors taking power directly from the engines. The scow was fitted with twin screws but only a single rudder, which could play havoc with navigation when the boat was in reverse. It didn't have much of a keel either and could slide sideways in a stiff crosswind, so the thrusters were needed for delicate manoeuvring around mussel rafts and functioned very well for the kind of work Pete was doing. Their effectiveness especially came to the fore during the Wellington Airport work that was coming up and as Pete says "they were worth their weight in gold".

In 1983 Peter started using the boat for putting down lines and anchor blocks for other mussel farmers in the Sounds. It became a much-appreciated pleasure craft for family and friends as well. It had high sides so it was ideal for the youngsters and there was plenty of open deck space for barbecuing and fishing.

In 1985, a truly remarkable piece of work came along. Severe storms had seriously damaged the seawall at the ocean end of Wellington Airport and the Ministry of Works had put out a tender to rebuild it. It was largely an issue of moving, placing and anchoring large rocks to the existing wall, but not many companies had either the expertise or the equipment to do it. Peter jumped at it and it would turn out to be another one of those singular moments in his career.

I knew I could do it because we'd been doing 12-tonne anchors in the mussel business and to me it was just a matter of numbers. So I sent in my quote and waited, and waited, and when I didn't hear anything back I got on to them and asked what was going on. Well it turned out that they didn't believe my numbers – I'd quoted $250,000, which was the biggest tender I'd ever put in by a long way, but the other two quotes were well over $2 million. Those numbers were also close to their own estimate and they just didn't believe that I could do it at my price. Well I managed to convince them that I could and they said okay and we got the job.

We took the Success *over to Wellington the next Sunday, tied it up and checked in to the Salvation Army hostel. Murray and a couple of mates were with me and our engineer was Jim Elkington, who was also a certified diver. I already had the specifications for the job and we got lucky with the weather so on the Monday morning we got stuck into it. Later that day I called one of the Ministry's engineering people to let them know we were on site and he said he'd get over that Thursday to sign the contracts and go over the job with us. By the time he got there on Thursday, we were done. He had a look at the work, made us move a couple of rocks – just for the sake of it I think – and that was that. That job taught me a lot – my*

*expenses were around ten grand and I'd pulled off a 250-grand
contract. I was chuffed.*

Murray remembers the job well. "It was a piece of cake actually. It
didn't take long – hole in the wharf, get a rock, take it out and drop it in
and wire it down, get another one – that was really all there was to it. The
Success made all the difference because we could manoeuvre so precisely
and Pete knew the boat so well – he could handle it like he was driving
his ute."

Chris Godsiff recalls when Pete took that job on. "We were a bit
pissed off that he was taking off across the Strait when we wanted some
work done and we ragged him a bit about it. Pete just said, 'Well you don't
pay as well as the Ministry of Works does,' and of course as it turned out
he was done and back within a week with a packet of dosh."

The Shop

Bruce Hearn had received licence Number 2 at the same time the Yealands got their first licence. Bruce was an accountant by trade and had
been joint CEO of Marlborough Electric Power. His grandfather and
great-grandfather had been deep-sea hard-hat divers and Bruce had
always been a fishing nut. He continued on with the mussels and eventually got into oysters and now owns and runs Tio Point Oysters. Bruce first
got to know Peter in 1973 when the Yealands family, Bert Batenburg and
Associated Fishermen of Nelson were pretty much the only players in the
game. The major switch from accounting to marine farming was easy for
Bruce. As he says, "I loved being on the water – hated being in the office."

The Yealands family was very helpful when I got started and
later I bought a lot of equipment from Peter and now and
then we'd get into the usual little arguments. I was getting my
floats elsewhere at the time and Peter would always be on to
me – "When are you going to buy some floats off me?" "When
you build some decent ones," I'd say and laugh. And once when
I actually did buy some floats, he crowed away, "I've got ya,
I've finally got ya." And there was the time early on when we

needed lights for our rafts – one white and one yellow per raft
I think, it may've been two each – anyway Peter found this guy
in Tawa that had them and he ordered 50 yellow and 50 white
and I said why did you get so many and he said, "Well I didn't
want him to think we were small time."

It was always a pleasure to go out there and I never had
a problem with him business-wise. There was some hearsay
going round like "Oh look out for that Peter Yealands, he's a bit
sharp" but I put that down to tall-poppyism and not much else.
Those that knew him and had dealings with him rarely had any
problems. If the gear he sold was wrong or broke or something,
he'd always replace it with few questions asked – and usually
only to find out why so he could do better the next time. In all
the years I dealt with him, I never ever had a problem – I can
still remember the phone number to the shop.

Son Aaron was growing up and had been around the mussel
business for most of his young days. After school he would often help
his granddad tying the short ropes for the mussel lines, but found he was
getting regularly quizzed by his granddad and uncles about what Peter
was up to and when Peter found out he said that's enough. Aaron went
on to work with Pete both building the floats and working the mussock-
knitting machine. "The knitting machine was very tricky work – one
mistake and the needles could ruin $1000 worth of material. That and
making mussel floats I'd be working twelve-hour shifts, six days a week,
noon to midnight. But Dad paid well."

When Marlborough farmer Terry Schwass began thinking about
mussels in the 70s, Peter was the first person he went to for advice. He'd
known Pete since the molasses-in-the-hay days and when things went
wrong, as they often did in those early times, Peter was always his sound-
ing board. Says Terry,

You'd come back from a week in the Sounds and all your spat
had died or something had gone really bloody wrong and you'd
think, Jesus, this is the end of the world and you'd go over

to Peter and have a two-hour session and you'd come out all
pumped up and ready to go again. He was as strong as a bloody
ox and he'd work 100 hours a week, week in week out and
still keep going, still keep grinning and still be able to think,
whereas the average guy would be out on their ear and moan-
ing their arse off. Pete was no. 8 wire technology at its best. You
could put him in any situation and he'd nut his way out of it.
He'd always go, "Where's your balls – if you haven't got it, then
bloody well make it."

Peter's not shifty or shady – he's a straight-up businessman.
But if you happen to get in his way you could get stomped on.
He's like a good All Black rucker: if you're going to lie on the
ball you might get hurt. Regardless of who it is he'll give them
a scrap – but win, lose or draw there'll be no malice. He's just
a unique bloke, and there are times even now when things get
a bit tight and I think, "I wonder what that whiskery bastard
would've thought about that?"

Not Just Mussels

The 80s also saw Peter add to his other business pursuits. He had started
Gravel Supplies Co. in Spring Creek, on which both Murray Mears and
Larry Collins worked with him. They had a quarry out near Tua Marina
and would screen the gravel in the Wairau, cart it back into town and sell
most of it to Firth Concrete. Aaron was growing up and one of his first
jobs working with his dad was driving for the gravel company. The business was never a huge money earner but it carried on for fifteen years or so
and was a regular revenue stream. It also was steady work for Aaron and
actually became his home for a while in his bachelor days. Aaron learnt
as he went repairing vehicles and when the mechanic left, Peter bought
Aaron a big box of tools for his twenty-first birthday and told him he
was now the mechanic. Peter told him if he had to do anything he wasn't
comfortable with, bring in someone to do it first time and make sure he
learnt it so he could do it himself next time around.

Another one of Peter and Murray's ventures was salmon farming.
The idea was to hatch salmon smolts and send them out to sea and then

catch the salmon coming back to spawn. They leased some land in Spring Creek on the Wairau and set up some salmon hatcheries. Spring Creek lived up to its name – it had very good spring water and was an ideal site for a hatchery. Peter knew the farmer who owned the land and arranged to lease a bit of it. The problem was they were having trouble getting the lease finalised but, in Peter's usual manner, they carried on anyway. They spent a lot of money developing the block, built plastic tanks, and all the while the lease application was still with the farmer's lawyers and the farmer was now demanding more and more as he saw how much development Peter was doing. Peter and Murray had put in a lot of time, money and effort but the lease demands were becoming, to Peter's eyes, unrealistic.

At this time, along comes this American-turned-Kiwi businessman Terry Shagin who wanted to float a company to farm salmon, which would become Regal Salmon. This was during the very heady days of the share market (before the crash) and I'd become an avid player in the market. Shagin was putting together a prospectus for the Initial Public Offering (IPO) and wanted to portray as full a package as possible for public investors. He had everything lined up except the start of the cycle, which was the hatchery which we had – sort of, if you ignored the lease issue. Shagin wanted to buy us out and thought he was dealing with a couple of hillbillies and made a really stupid offer. So we thought, "Well we'll show him" and we went to work playing back and forth and the price went higher and higher. All the while, Shagin wanted to get his IPO prospectus printed and we were holding it up, resulting in him losing his cool with lost tempers on phone calls. In the meantime, Murray and I thought that offers like this don't come along too often and we did a deal with him – and it was a marvellous deal. We got so many shares free with options to buy more at half price. Regal Salmon was floated and listed in 1986, Shagin sorted out the lease situation and Murray and I walked away very very happy.

Larry Collins remembers another one of Peter's wilder schemes.

"Pete told us we were going to get into the geese market. He'd seen these geese that had been wandering around for years in some paddocks just south of Havelock so Peter got on to the farmer and the farmer said, 'Yeah you can have 'em'. So there we are running around these paddocks with fishing nets chasing and catching hundreds of these bloody geese. The idea was we'd pluck them and sell them but they were just tough as old boots. We didn't sell too many of them."

Another venture that didn't work out, although through no fault of his own, was when Peter decided to go gold mining on the Wakamarina River, north of Havelock. Gold had been found in the Wakamarina River but not a lot and not for a long time. Peter thought there was still some more to be had and put a plan together, which would include using the *Success,* and duly applied for a licence to dredge the river. Needless to say his licence application caught the attention of the Havelock locals in a big way. Although the venture would provide jobs and income for the area, there were the usual complaints from the greenies and the NIMBYs (not in my back yard) versus the support of many business people who saw the venture as a good thing for the town. A meeting was called in Canvastown just outside of Havelock and the hall was bursting with concerned citizens – about half for and half against Peter's application. It caused a huge and well-publicised uproar and divided the town for a while. It wasn't the first time or the last time that some scheme of Peter's would rattle the locals. And although you wouldn't really call him ruthless, he knew that this sort of thing went with the territory and he developed quite a thick skin over the years. Eventually he got a licence but it turned out to be a sop to both sides. It was only for six months, where normally they would be for twenty years or so. No gold extraction process was going to be built in half a year so the venture never got going and nobody won.

Magic Carpet Ride
Peter would have to find his gold elsewhere and as it happened Rogernomics was about to be unleashed on the New Zealand public. After the 1984 election, Finance Minister Roger Douglas, in the newly formed Labour Government of David Lange, began to hastily reform the New Zealand economy. The speed of the reforms was later explained in Douglas's book

Unfinished Business: "Define your objectives clearly, and move towards them in quantum leaps, otherwise the interest groups will have time to mobilise and drag you down."[4] The financial market was deregulated and controls on foreign exchange removed. Many subsidies were removed or significantly reduced, as was tariff protection, the marginal tax rate was halved over a number of years from 66 per cent to 33 per cent and the GST was introduced. With no restrictions on overseas money coming into the country the focus in the economy shifted from the productive sector to the finance sector. It was open season and the share market craze began.

Investors flooded the share market after the deregulation and huge fortunes were made. Thousands of ordinary New Zealanders had exploited their sudden freedom from strict government control over economic activity and started buying and selling shares on the stock market. Always on the lookout for financial gain, Peter became an avid player and was quite vocal to his mates about the gains to be made. Bruce Hearn recalls dropping into Peter's shop to buy gear and Peter would regale him with stories and exhortations. "Now I'm a CA and was a bit more fiscally conservative than Peter, but he'd always be on to me – When are you going to buy in, got a hot deal on this one, and so forth. The whole country just sort of got mesmerised by the share market. And he'd always be on to me and I'd keep saying, 'Peter it can't last – it's all bullshit – you've got to look at dividend yield – if they're not performing on that, it's all hype' and we'd have these friendly arguments back and forth. And for ages I couldn't go in there without getting into these discussions."

Peter had started with a relatively modest investment of $50,000, which he grew into a $5 million portfolio over the next year and a half. The growth was indicative of both Peter's business acumen and the staggering growth of the market at that time. Peter also recalls that he was now becoming noticed in the higher echelons of New Zealand business and was being treated, as he says, "like an institution" and was being offered shares and information that had not yet filtered out to regular folk. Peter had a good relationship with several large brokerage houses and

4. Douglas, Roger, *Unfinished Business*, Random House NZ Ltd, 1993.

things were looking very rosy. At the same time, he urged two young local stockbrokers to set up their own company, which became Marlborough Sharebrokers. They agreed to broker Peter for 1 per cent of all his share market activities, which was a good deal for both parties – low rates for Peter and Peter's sizeable share activity for them. It also came to light after the crash that they had been mirroring most of Peter's activity with their own buys and sells, mostly buys in those days. In the family, Peter, Vai, and Aaron and Peter's mates Murray Mears and Larry Collins all had a share portfolio. Gains were tax-free and a splendid time was had by all. They were wild times and Peter recalls that "You really had to be stupid to lose money on the share market."

Of course Bruce Hearn was right and after a period of sustained growth, the Wall Street market in New York dropped sharply in October 1987. And what felt like ripples elsewhere was a tidal wave in New Zealand. On 25 October Peter received a phone call from his major broker in Wellington advising him to sell everything he had. Peter called his local boys and told them to sell everything he had listed with them. Of course they ditched their own holdings first and Peter came second on that transaction. But the early warning was not early enough and Peter's holdings went down with everyone else's.

Peter lost $5 million dollars that day – pretty much everything that he'd made in the market. He feels he didn't get badly burned: he hadn't been borrowing or mortgaging the farm as many did to play the market, and he looks back on it as "a wonderful experience". His Regal Salmon shares were victims but little of his actual own money was involved and when the dust settled he was pretty much back to where he started. Peter still holds shares in some companies. Some acquired through business deals and some that fell through the cracks in the crash and missed getting sold, and he has been a long-time part-owner of Flat Creek Coal in Murchison. He never played the market again – until Oyster Bay came along, but more of that later.

The Maya

In the mid 80s, Peter saw an ad for a 50ft concrete-hulled schooner called the *Maya* that was berthed in Lyttelton Harbour, south of Christchurch.

It had been built by a Dutch immigrant boat builder and was based on the design of the iconic Slocum's *Spray*. Joshua Slocum was a Canadian-American seaman and adventurer who had built the *Spray* from an abandoned oyster boat in Massachusetts in the late 1890s and then proceeded to sail it around the world. The design has fostered many copies and is recognised for its stable nature and its ability to steer itself on downwind legs by adjusting only the sails and without touching the helm. These capabilities – whether inherent or not in this ferro-cement-hulled copy is not known – were about to be tested by a gang of mad Kiwi blokes led by Peter. He and Murray Mears purchased the boat and Larry Collins also ended up with a third share. The plan was to sail it up to Picton and fit it out for pleasure boating, but first they had to pick up the boat.

Peter, Murray and Larry travelled to Christchurch, where they spent a few days cleaning and kitting it out. They were soon joined by half a dozen mates, including his brother Stephen, who'd rented a car and driven down to join the party cruise. Brother Kevin had also been invited but knowing full well his susceptibility to sea-sickness he passed on the trip – and just as well, as it turned out. Food and grog were loaded on board along with their navigation equipment, which consisted of a hand-held compass and a few charts. Pete's experience of sailing boats was nil, but he'd done what he usually did when confronted with a new challenge: do a bit of research and jump in. Finally all the preparations had been made and it was time to set off.

> *The weather in Lyttelton that day was complete rubbish and we waited and waited. I finally went and talked to a fisherman who said, "If you keep waiting, you'll never go," so we decided to head out. It was late afternoon and there was a southerly building but I'd been to the library and read a couple of books about sailing so I thought, "We'll be right." The boat had a little Perkins diesel auxiliary engine that hung off the side with long flapping v-belts driving the prop, and enough sail to get us going so we headed out of the harbour running on the motor and out into open water. We immediately caught a really strong southerly, got the mainsails up but then the main boom promptly broke. We rushed around and managed to jury-rig*

the boom back into sort-of working order and in an hour or so we roughly learned to sail.

The DIY sailors had managed to get a little foresail up so they were moving along but Pete had always been told that in bad weather you're safer out to sea than near the coast so they headed straight out toward the Chathams. It was now getting dark and the only outside lights on the boat were some Tilley kerosene navigation lamps. They had three of them so the third one they used to read their compass, which sat on a box at the helm. But then a couple of big waves broke over the stern and wiped that lamp out so now they could only see the compass by lightning flashes, of which there were many.

The storm was really blowing now and I confess to being a little worried out there but I can tell you the only place I wanted to be was on the tiller. It was a mess down below because pretty well everyone else was seasick and there was an unholy mess of beer, food, vomit, and all made worse with diesel fumes – it was just disgusting so Murray and Larry and I stayed up top. Well it was a ride. We were dead abeam to those waves and they weren't small. The boat was wide and squat and heavy with only about a foot of freeboard on it and we were taking on a fair bit of water. The boat was shuddering on every wave – up one side and then hammered down on the next. It being our first time out on the boat, we just didn't know what it was capable of and it was getting very very scary. We lost all our storm sails – they all blew out so all we had now was this little auxiliary motor which was heating up so we knocked that back to where it wouldn't overheat and just kept trying to keep abeam to the sea.

During the night, they came upon a fleet of Japanese squid boats that were all hove to on their drogues. Fortunately they saw the *Maya* and shone their spotlights so that Pete and crew could manoeuvre through them. About an hour later, a SafeAir mail plane flew over them and put a spotlight on them. SafeAir already knew they were out there but Pete didn't know whether to wave or not. He figured if he waved, they might think everything was okay but it wasn't so he didn't do anything.

But I guess we'd made some decent headway because when the morning came it was calm and sunny and we couldn't see any land. What we could see was that the boat was completely covered with seabirds. They were on the masts, the cabin top, everywhere, so I guess the storm had knackered them as well as us. At any rate, we reckoned our best move was to turn around and head back the way we came. So we managed to get a couple of sails up that we'd repaired and after about two hours we finally saw land. We all felt a lot better now and while the boys started cleaning up the mess below, we headed up the coast and around Cape Campbell in pretty good time. We trolled some lines out the back and caught some kahawai and mackerel. Things were slowly returning to normal. We sailed into Port Underwood that evening, put the anchor down for the first time and had a good feed of steak and fish and a good night's sleep.

The next morning we sailed out of Port Underwood and now we were feeling very good about the boat. We had it leaned over with the sails taut and it was just lovely. We all felt we were true sailors then, standing out there on deck looking up at the sails with big silly grins on our faces – it was magic. We sailed into the Tory Channel and headed for Picton and I guess word had got out too because there must have been twenty or thirty boats that came and met us and we had quite an escort coming into Picton. One of the boys had for some reason brought along several pairs of ladies' knickers and hung them off the boom, and we had a beer or two on the way in. It was a lot of fun. And to top things off, there was a big gang on the jetty as well, who gave us a big wave when we came in, so it was a nice ending to a pretty wild trip. I can bet that for most of us on that trip, myself included, it was one of the best adventures of our lives.

The plan now was to refurbish the boat and make it into a first-rate pleasure craft. The original cabin was quite claustrophobic so they built a new and enlarged one. The engine room was also cheek by jowl with the galley and they sorted that out too. But despite the best laid plans all three of them were just too busy to get really stuck in with the refurbishment and it was causing a bit of friction. And so before friendships were lost they decided the best thing to do was sell the vessel, which they did and made a few dollars on it as well. The *Maya* can still be seen from time to time in Ngakuta Bay in the Queen Charlotte Sound.

Timber to Taiwan

By 1986 Peter was avidly playing the share market. Industrial Marine was ticking along nicely and the Mud Bay property that he had started developing was shaping up well. Life was looking good.

One day he was working in his shop making floats when a sparkling new Porsche rolled up with a beautiful blonde in the passenger seat. The small-town lads working there were suitably impressed – this was quite an event at the shop. Everyone stopped to look – at both the Porsche and the blonde – and out from the driver's seat hopped a handsome, suntanned bloke. "Pete, me old mate, how ya doing? It's been years since I've seen you. It's Dan, Dan Summers." They shook hands and Peter finally recognised him. They'd known each other a few years back, though Peter wouldn't have thought of him as a close mate. With the lovely blonde, Dan's wife, they sat down to coffee and started talking. Dan was telling Peter about all the fantastic opportunities in the Asian market for timber and Peter was soon swept away with the stories from this enthusiastic and apparently well-off businessman. The idea was to harvest timber, mostly radiata, and beech when they could get it, and ship it to Taiwan, where Summers had his contacts. Within a week they'd formed a partnership, calling it Tai-Swiss, with the deal being that Peter had the money and local knowledge and Dan had the overseas contacts. Like anything Pete got involved in, he was into it full-bore and they were soon making a lot of noise about this new business venture. The company had the usual growing pains one would expect but it picked up and over the next two years became a reasonably successful operation.

Larry Collins was working for Peter at the time and remembers carting wood out of Robin Hood Bay and from a lot of farms in the Rai

Valley area. Most of it was trucked over to Picton and then shipped out to Taiwan. When the company first got going, they needed some special equipment and of course with Pete it was a case of making it themselves. Larry recalls:

> Pete taught me to weld then. He was always dreaming up these different bits of equipment that we'd need to get a job done. So when he started Tai-Swiss he said we needed a logging trailer and he'd show me how to build it. I said, "Me – are you sure – they gotta be done properly don't they?" and he said, "No, no, you'll be right" so we built this thing. Pete was there showing me what to do and we got this big trailer built and it didn't look too bad actually. Of course, we had to get an engineer to make sure it was okay because we were going to be using it on the roads. Anyway the engineer checked it out and said, "Yeah good as gold" and away we went. I couldn't believe it – here we'd built this logging trailer, road-worthy and everything.

> *As the business expanded, we started exporting radiata logs through Elders Forestry in Invercargill and Elders liked what they saw. Good contacts, good work, etc. – they just liked the package and said they'd like to be a partner. They were a pretty big player and we thought it would be a good fit. The share market had just crashed and I was quite open to the idea, as you can imagine. So we sat down, hammered out a deal that would work for both us and them and away we went. Elders Forestry became the working partner, Elders Finance would put up the money and all of the legal business and paperwork was done up in less than three months.*

> *It was going pretty good to start with – Elders made the first two payments due to us, and then for some reason they pulled the bloody plug on us. It certainly seemed like a dramatic policy shift overnight and left everyone in the lurch. I was not impressed. Elders knew upfront that the thing was going to take a year or so to get going as this had been discussed, but nevertheless they got cold feet and pulled out. I guess I was probably the big loser in the whole*

thing. I tried to make sure that everyone got paid, but I was a little slow in getting my own bills and paperwork in and was last in the queue when Elders Finance cut us off. It took the best part of two years but everyone got paid – except for me and I reckoned I lost somewhere around a hundred grand.

A Bitter Blow

A constant through Peter's business endeavours in the 1980s was Industrial Marine. He had expanded his inventory, was manufacturing floats, mussock, anchors and was doing a lot of contracting with the *Success*, putting in longlines for both his partner company, Pelorus Aquaculture, and many other farmers in the Sounds. But his biggest customer was still his family.

Keith, Kevin and Stephen had grown Marlborough Mussel Co. into an ever-expanding and profitable enterprise. They could be quite secretive at times and never joined any associations but their advances in farming methodology, allied with Keith's indomitable will, were a potent combination. When they built the *Coutanui* it had perhaps the most sophisticated harvesting system at the time and they were relentless in expanding and putting money back into the business. By 1990, MMC was the largest of the independents and though Keith shunned official groups and meetings, he and Dorrie were by all accounts a quiet inspiration to many of the other farmers.

Before they were done, they had six vessels operating and over twenty employees, not counting themselves. They paid well and paid promptly and Keith recalls that through their bonus system many of the workers were making over $1000 a week, which was good money at the time. In the early 90s MMC sold a 35 per cent share of their company to Pacifica Seafoods and eventually sold the remainder to them in 1998. At the time of sale, MMC owned fifty farms and managed another twenty-five. The price was rumoured to be $27 million and Keith recounts a telling tale: "We were already partners with Pacifica and they had asked what my selling price was for the company so I told them. A few days later, a young lawyer or accountant – something like that – calls me and says, 'Yeah we'd like to do this, so let's set up a meeting and discuss it,' and I say, 'What's to discuss' and he says, 'Well we have to work the numbers, negotiate, that sort of thing.' And I say, 'We don't need a meeting, and there's nothing to negotiate – you know my price and that's the price.'" The deal was done shortly after that, and of course at Keith's price. Sir Clifford Skeggs of Pacifica had this to say: "Keith Yealands was always a wise old head, and under his leadership they learned to be very successful growers indeed and kept doing it." The final feather in the cap for Keith Yealands was being awarded an OBE, about which he says, "Yeah – that was a bit of a shock wasn't it?"

But before all this, the rift between Peter and his brothers would explode again, with much worse consequences than before. Since Peter had left New Zealand Marine Culture, their relationship had almost returned to normal. The brothers had been invited along for the *Maya* trip and Kevin, being an accredited mechanic, recalls Pete asking him for advice when he built his first float machine. But by 1986 there were rumblings within MMC to build their own equipment. It had always been how they liked to do things and Kevin was lobbying Keith about it. Keith recalls, "We always bought from Pete, keep it in the family you know, and while all this was going on Kevin would be saying, 'Why the hell don't we make our own floats. I can jack it all up,' and I'd say, 'Well no, Peter's making them, he's in the family.'" But Kevin didn't let go and it soon escalated.

MMC was still a good customer, buying a lot of floats from me, but one day when I wasn't there my brothers came over and one of them started chatting with Larry out front while the other one started measuring up my gyro-spinner. When I heard about it, I was f***ing wild and went over to talk to them. They said, "Well, Pete, we did give you some ideas about the whole thing when you were building it so it's not as if we know nothing about it." I says, "You could've asked because what you're doing is f***ing industrial spying and it's just not on." And they said, "Well don't worry about it – we're only going to make these floats for ourselves and won't be in competition with your business. And by the way, we know that you sold some floats to someone else cheaper than what you sold them to us," which was *true. Needless to say things went downhill from there and within three months they were selling to everyone. From that point on, it was them and us. They were just a few hundred yards up the road making floats flat out, capturing the Yealands name and selling in opposition to me. I used to send a monthly newsletter to my customers and in it I'd refer to them as "the others", so it was quite a public spat.*

Keith had acquiesced. "I said to Kevin, 'You go ahead and make them – get the machine and we'll make our own floats'. It was just for us to start with, but eventually he had three machines and a bloke full-time and he was making floats and we were selling them in opposition to Pete and the business just grew quite steadily. That didn't make any bad blood I don't think, not that I knew at any rate."

As with many family disputes, the final straw is invariably something small; something which by itself would not be a big issue but when tempers are running hot, it never takes much to light the fuse. What was very sad about the final disagreement was that it wasn't between Peter and his brothers, it was between him and his parents. Keith remembers it well.

Peter was making the mussel stockings as well and we bought them off him. Kevin said he wanted to get our own machine and I said, "No, we'll buy them off Pete," but we had to take a batch back one day, wrong size or amount or something like that, and Mum and I took it back. We thought it was twelve cartons or whatever it was and Peter refused and said we'd only had ten. And I said, "Peter, your Mum and I don't have to try and beat anybody down, we don't do that." I said, "If we say we brought so many cartons back that's what we brought back". But Pete says, "No – his chap was making the stocking and said he'd never made that many and I believe him," and I said, "All right," but I guess it wasn't. We got some machines from Italy and we made our own. When we finished up we had most of the stocking business – we had six machines and a bloke working full-time, but whether that rankled Pete I don't know – it was never mentioned.

But it rankled, and rankled badly. What started with floats for their own company's use, then selling them to everyone, followed by a silly argument over a couple of cartons of stocking, split the family apart. It would take many years for the wounds to heal and the scars were deep. It would seem that Keith was never fully aware of the depth of Peter's anger and Peter didn't see the need to try to explain or apologise. Brothers being brothers, the twins probably were aware of Pete's resentment but they were just as ambitious as Peter and had dug their heels in.

My biggest regret and what is the worst business mistake I ever made was regarding my brothers. The family was my biggest customer and they got the best price for stocking, floats, etc. As my operation became more efficient I was able to buy in bigger quantities and lower my margins. And then at one point, another big customer came along and I really wanted his business and I'd worked out a very good price – lower than what I was charging the family – and I made the mistake of not offering the same lower price to them. Of course they found out and that's when the fight started. The other thing was the day when Kevin and Steve did the float spying thing when I wasn't there, and that was a red flag to me. The low price issue I admit was a business mistake but there was no malice attached to it. The float spying was different and I've never really forgiven them for that.

The family feud that evolved from the mussel business deeply affected Vai. To this day, she still often refers to Keith and Dorrie as Mr and Mrs Yealands and it is obvious that there was a lot of pain for her. She can remember taking the kids over to Keith and Dorrie's and saying, "You may have your differences with Peter, but these are your grandchildren and your arguments have nothing to do with them." It got to the point where Pete and Vai and the kids would have their own Christmas dinner and would only drop by to see Pete's mum and dad for a quick early drink. Finally one Christmas, Dorrie made the gesture to invite them to stay for dinner. Peter wasn't too keen, but Vai recalls saying to him, "That was a long walk for her to come across the room and ask us," and so they stayed but it was not comfortable. Someone took a photo of everyone and Vai remembers thinking that it was a good thing that they got a picture – and it turned out to be the last time for a long time that the whole family was together. While it was a very painful period, both Peter and Vai have let time heal the wounds as best as possible. In 2004, their old friend Jim Jenkins told them that a book was being written about the industry (Carol Dawber's book *Lines in the Water*) and suggested this was Peter's opportunity to set the record straight on the whole issue, but Peter declined. Vai feels that the people they worked with in the industry were aware of what really happened and that is sufficient.

Time for a change

The 1980s were a wild ride for Peter. Ventures started – some went well, others didn't, some made sense, others…well. He refined his manufacturing techniques, rebuilt two vessels, confirmed his potential for taking on huge jobs and succeeding, and took a ride on the share market roller coaster. Industrial Marine became a solid money-earner but at the same time was the crucible of a bitter family fight that took years to heal. At the end of the decade, Aaron was twenty and Danielle a teenager. He and Vai had a lovely house and Pete was also developing some property at Mud Bay in the Pelorus Sound. He had become interested in deer farming and planting trees. It was time for a change.

> *Sometime in 1989 I had my best month ever – took in around $500,000 – and I said to Vai, "Well, it's been a good ten years; I've been going flat-out seven days a week, the kids can't use the phone because there's always customers and what not calling, so I'm happy to get out of this." I rang up a real estate agent to put the business on the market. It sold very quickly for a good price to a group of investors headed by Jack Goldsmith, an accountant with quite a good reputation, and the agent told me he got more goodwill from that than any other business he'd sold at the time. There were ten shareholders who were buying it but on the day they were to close, two shareholders pulled out and they said, "Peter, we want you to take those shares and be a director of the company." I didn't really have*

any option on this if I wanted the deal closed so I ended up retaining shares.

The new owners changed the name of the company and all had agreed that Peter would at some point build a new plant for them. This was okay with Pete because he didn't really want them in his back yard. They had a plan to put up a new building quite a way out of town, but six weeks later Pete was woken up at 2 o'clock one morning by a raging fire behind his house and it was the factory. What was essentially a plastics factory with millions of dollars worth of gear full of plastic, gas ovens and cotton bins went up like a torch. The factory was burned to the ground.

As a result of all that, I ended up putting up a building in town on the east side of Grove Road and leased it to them. I was still a share-holder and they asked me to manage the company for a while and get it back to a somewhat normal operation with an eye to selling it. I did and we sold to a bloke in Picton that did very well with it. It changed hands again to someone who split the retail side off from the manufacturing. The larger part of that building I revamped and subdivided it and rented it out. Subsequently I sold the main build-ing. Commercial development was pretty good money, but it was boring stuff. I did it for a year or so but it just wasn't me. I needed a change.

Top left: Peter's father, Trooper Keith Yealands, aged 19, in 1940.

Yealands family

Bottom left: Peter's mum, Doris (Dorrie) Davies, aged 18, in 1941.

Yealands family

Top right: The iconic Long Range Desert Group (LRDG), T1 patrol, in North Africa, 1942. Keith Yealands is at the top on the right.

Yealands family

Bottom right: Keith and Dorrie Yealands' wedding, December 1945, in Blenheim.   Yealands family

Top left: Pete's twin brothers with a very large snapper at Moenui Bay, c. 1956. Yealands family

Top right: Peter, left, at nine months, with sister Sue – his first known "wetlands" development.
Yealands family

Middle: The Yealands children, 1955. *L to R*: Sue, the twins Stephen and Kevin, and Peter, aged seven.
Yealands family

Bottom: Whitney Street School, Blenheim, c. 1954. Peter is second from the left, in the second row from the top.
Yealands family

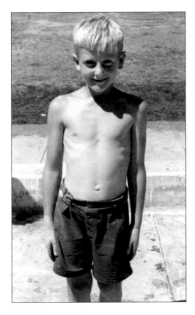

Top right: Peter at 15 with his beloved Buick. Yealands family

Bottom right: Peter aged 17, off D'Urville Island on the *Belfast* with Tiri Elkington.
Yealands family

Top left: Peter aged 10 – casually dressed as usual. Yealands family

Bottom left: Peter at 14 at home in Blenheim with a feline friend.
Yealands family

Left: Pete, left, and two mates at the Grovetown dance the night before he met Vai. January 1968.

Yealands family

Right: Pete and Vai's wedding at Church of the Nativity in Blenheim, 3 August 1968.

Yealands family

Top left: First mussel rafts loaded. Pete's brother Stephen, left, and friend Murray Mears keep a close eye. Yealands family

Top right: The first ferro-concrete mussel raft – built by the Yealands family. Yealands family

Bottom: Participants of a 1973 mussel farming meeting in Blenheim, arranged by the Fisheries Industry Board (FIB). *L to R*: Don Jamieson, Marlborough harbourmaster; Peter Yealands; Philip Tortell, Victoria University Marine Laboratory; Jim Jenkins, FIB; Bert Batenburg, Havelock; Peter Chapman, FIB asstistant general manager. Marlborough Express

Middle: A big improvement with the polystyrene pontoons built by the Yealands family. Yealands family

Top: Early pre-longline mussel rafts in Mills Bay, built by NZ Marine Culture, the Yealands family company.

Yealands family

Top middle: Peter's Industrial Marine Ltd (IML) "factory" at Grovetown, where over 200,000 floats were made.

Yealands family

Bottom middle: A cargo of IML floats – the precarious load behind the family car is indicative of the DIY nature of early mussel farming.

Yealands family

Bottom: Running out the longlines on hundreds of Peter's floats.

Yealands family

vi

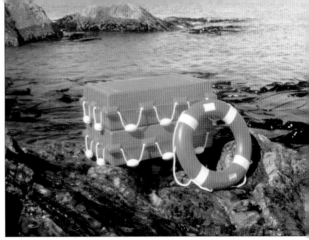

Top left: Keith Yealands at work. Keith was over 50 when he started mussel farming. Yealands family

Top right: Safety equipment that Peter also manufactured at Industrial Marine Ltd. Yealands family

Middle left: Massive 12-tonne anchor blocks built by Peter at IML for the longlines. The experience building them paved the way for his success on the Wellington Airport job. Yealands family

Middle right: A floating jetty built by Peter, heading for Picton.
Yealands family

Above: Brothers Stephen and Kevin after they formed Marlborough Mussel Co. with father Keith.
Yealands family

Top left: Keith Yealands receives his OBE from Governor-General Dame Catherine Tizard. Yealands family

Top right: Peter and Vai, Christmas 1992 at Grovetown. Yealands family

Middle: The Grovetown house under construction, with son Aaron in front of the infamous swimming pool, in 1978. Yealands family

Bottom: The Grovetown house was completed in 1979 and the family could finally move out of the caravan where they'd lived for two years. Yealands family

Top left: Peter, a happy man, at
Kaiuma Station, c. 1995.

Yealands family

Top right: Danielle and Aaron,
Christmas 1992.

Yealands family

Middle: Keith and Dorrie Yealands,
Christmas 1992.

Yealands family

Bottom: Pete weighing deer antlers
at Kaiuma Station.

Yealands family

Above: One of Peter's beautiful wetlands at the North Bank vineyard, 2000. Yealands family

Below: A stunning view of wetlands at Seaview with Mount Tapuaenuku ("Mount Tapi") in the background.

Yealands family

Top: Wetland development at the Seaview vineyard, 2004.

Yealands family

Middle: Vineyard development at Seaview, 2004.

Yealands family

Bottom: View back to Kaiuma Station in 2009 from the Kaiuma Park Estates development.

Tom Percy

Top: Son Aaron with a young owl found abandoned in the vineyard and adopted by the maintenance crew.

Tom Percy

Bottom: Daughter Danielle Yealands, 2011.

Tom Percy

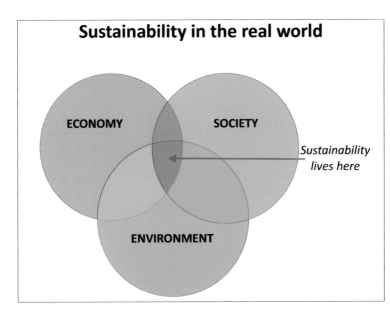

Sustainability in the real world

ECONOMY

SOCIETY

Sustainability lives here

ENVIRONMENT

Top: Sustain-ability model – a guideline for all Yealands staff.

Tom Percy

Bottom: The scow *Success* shortly after Peter sold the boat to Rob Pooley, 1990.

Rob Pooley

Top: Kaiuma Station in 2009: view of cleared paddocks. Tom Percy

Bottom: Pete and Vai with the first run of Full Circle wine in plastic bottles. Jim Tannock

Top left: Babydoll sheep (happy and smiling) at Yealands Estate vineyard. Jim Tannock

Top right: Not an uncommon sight at Yealands Estate is the boss mucking in with some of his favourite native plants.
Jim Tannock

Bottom: Wetlands and birds at Yealands Estate.
Jim Tannock

The Yealands Estate Cellar Door, with the matai floor made from Kaiuma Station trees. Jim Tannock

The Yealands Estate Winery at Seaview – the North Island can be seen in the background. Jim Tannock

CHAPTER SEVEN

The Greening of Peter Yealands

I wanted to build a park that a King would want to buy.

As was noted at the beginning of chapter four, Peter always had many things on the go at the same time. This chapter starts chronologically from the same point as the previous one, but looks at Peter's evolution in the sustainable working of the land. All that follows leads to where he is today. It will become clear that Peter's belief and commitment to sustainability within a viable and profitable business environment did not happen overnight.

In the thirty years since he started working the land, he has cleared and made productive thousands of hectares, planted tens of thousands of trees, stood the viticulture industry on its head, done the David and Goliath thing, won awards and become an icon of sustainable business practices. He has taken his mental bulldozer, climbed to the top of the scruffiest, stoniest, most gorse-infested unworkable pile of dirt he could find and quietly said, "I'll show you."

Mud Bay

In 1981 Peter had become interested in both deer farming and forestry and a particular block of land caught his eye – a 283ha property at Mud Bay in the Pelorus Sound, which he purchased. He knew the area well, both the waters of the Pelorus Sound from his mussel farming work and inland from many weekends spent pig-hunting in the area.

Mud Bay had originally been called Rimu Bay but extensive logging many years before had silted up the bay and the name was changed accordingly. This didn't please Vai Yealands at all and she always preferred to call it Rimu Bay. When Peter obtained the property, there were still remnants of old boilers and other milling equipment left over from the Brownlee foresting empire at the end of the nineteenth century.

Peter's plan was to develop the property for both deer and forestry farming and to build a house and settle there. There was no access by road at the time, which didn't please Vai as she never liked the combination of water and small boats. She remembers that they didn't have a very big boat at the time and it could be a treacherous trip from Havelock to the property. After a particularly nasty trip back, she laid down the law and told Peter to either get a bigger boat or she'd never go there again. Peter did get a bigger boat but as Vai says, "The glory was gone".

Peter's work at Mud Bay is significant for three reasons which have gone on to become consistent factors in his life. Mud Bay started his serious interest in deer farming, which has continued and still goes on at Kaiuma Station. He got to know and love big tractors, diggers and bulldozers and became hooked on what he calls "land sculpture". And perhaps most importantly, he started planting trees. In fact he remembers the length of time he spent at Mud Bay not by the age of his children but by the age of the first pine trees he planted there.

When Peter purchased the property in 1981 he had no real experience with large earthmoving equipment and originally had a contractor come in to start the roads for the property. He remembers ringing the chap who said it was too wet, which Pete couldn't understand because it was a bright sunny day and hadn't been raining. The contractor explained to him that the ground was too wet and it took a bit of convincing to convey that he knew what he was talking about. He explained that the problem was the undergrowth under the pig fern, where layers of dense vegetation build up and act like a sponge. When you get these big machines on it they just slide around, with the undergrowth getting caught up in the tracks. Pete was always listening and learning and a short while later he bought his first bulldozer, a small Allis-Chalmers with a GM motor. His early learning curve of big diggers was somewhat accelerated by the speed at which he seemed to go through machines. The Allis-Chalmers exploded early on when the motor raced away on him, burnt all the oil in the sump and revved until it disintegrated. Then he bought a couple of Caterpillar D7's, one good one and one for spare parts, and now he was in business, for a while anyway.

I stopped one day at lunchtime to eat and looked back and there was smoke coming out of the bloody thing. All the dried-out fern had got caught up between the manifold and the motor and caught on fire. I thought it was just smouldering so I put my hands in to brush it away and of course got my hands burned and by then it was too late anyway and it ended up burning to the ground. After that I got a Cat D5B, which was a beautiful little tractor and much more modern. I bought that from a bloke in Blenheim who'd rolled it but it was still in pretty good nick and I took that down to Mud Bay and really got clearing land with that.

But not without incident. One day he was pushing down a steep hill and the blade on the front instead of digging in and clearing slipped up over the soggy undergrowth and suddenly Pete found his tracks on a mess of very wet fern. There was nothing to hold it and the tractor took off downhill with Pete on it, not knowing whether to jump or stay on. He could see that there was a small bit of level ground at the bottom and then a steep drop-off. So what should he do – save himself for sure but probably lose the tractor or stay on and see if he could save both? In the end he stayed on. The ground did level out a bit and Pete managed to stop the tractor, but when he tried to find some better ground and reverse it back up the hill, it was no go. There he was, stuck on a little plateau with a steep greasy hill behind him and a sheer drop in front of him.

I thought first off I'd leave it there for a week until it dried out, because there was a bit of a track from where I'd slid down the hill. But it never dried out properly so I went down there with an end- less chain, a crowbar, a sledgehammer and a shovel. I went about ten paces up the hill and dug in a big post and used the chain to winch the thing up with the tractor idling in gear to give it a bit of pull. Between me winching and the tractor idling in gear, it slowly

*inched up the hill. When I got it up there, I dug another hole and
repeated the process and I finally got it up but it took me ages to get
that thing out of there. I could have hired another bulldozer, brought
it out by barge and used it to tow mine out, but I reckoned it would
run to two or three grand and I didn't have that sort of money in
those days, so another lesson learnt. I guess that contracting bloke I
first spoke to knew what he was talking about.*

Over the first year Peter had done a lot of clearing, had put in extensive deer fencing and soon had 20 hectares of cleared deer paddocks and
had built a little shed to sleep in, as he was mostly on his own out there.
The difficulty was getting back and forth to the property, which was
exacerbated by the lack of any decent landing and loading facility on the
property. There was still no road access and all haulage was done by John-
sons Barge from Havelock. That was straightforward enough but once
the barge got to Mud Bay there was no easy way to get trucks off it and
onto the farm. It made for a slow and difficult process, compounded by
the ever-present gorse, and he needed some method of clear access into
the farm.

He knew what he was looking for, kept his eyes open and finally
came across an old 100ft barge up at Wakatahuri that he reckoned would
make a pretty good jetty for the property and so he bought it. But as
always there were some things to get sorted. The barge was chocka with
worm so the first thing Peter did was run it up the Pelorus River into
fresh water, where he cut a section out of the side and sank it to get rid
of the worm. From there he towed it out to Mud Bay and sited it where
the Havelock barge could run right up against the end of it and the trucks
could then be driven straight off the Havelock barge onto his new jetty
and up the road to the deer farm. But once again Pete's activities attracted
the attention of the authorities.

*I'd put in a lot of roading on the site and wanted to gravel them
as best I could. There was a bit of gravel on the site and a lot of it
on the beach so I'd take that up and spread it on the roads. I had
a little digger and truck and one day I was working away at this*

and noticed a large boat come into the bay and drop off someone in a little dinghy. The dinghy threw out an anchor and this bloke was sitting in it and I assumed he was going to do some fishing – there was lots of snapper in the bay and people fishing weren't uncommon. But then I saw a reflection from what I reckoned were binoculars, so I got my binoculars out and there was this bloke watching me. Well I wondered what the hell that was about, but he didn't move and I got on with the work.

Towards the end of the day after I'd brought up maybe twenty or thirty loads he comes ashore and says he's so-and-so from Department of Conservation and asks me what I'm doing. So I says, "I'm just gravelling my roads," which he bloody knew because he'd been watching me for hours. And so he says, "You can't do that, you're taking gravel off the beach," and I says, "Well look there was a lot of rain last week and it washed the gravel off my land and I'm just putting it back." I know that sounds a bit cheeky but it was sort of true, there had been a big flood and it washed a lot of gravel down to the beach but this bloke wasn't buying it. He says he's going to do a report on this and I says, "For f**k sake, mate, you've been sitting out there all bloody day watching me do it, if you were genuinely concerned why didn't you come and stop me right at the start? If you pop me now you're just being bloody hypocritical." Anyway he retaliated with a few words and buggered off.

A few weeks later Peter received a notice in the mail from DOC threatening to prosecute him so he went and explained the situation to them. He explained that he was trying to make a living with his deer farm down there and if there was any concern they should've spoken to him at the start rather than wait all day. As it turned out, they were sympathetic and understood what he was trying to do. Pete managed to talk them into letting him build a road right along the seacoast on DOC land so that he could build his jetty and have access. He did all that, but still ended up going to court because the first bloke had also passed on the complaint to the harbour master about the jetty and now he wanted to have a go at Peter.

*Well the way it worked out, I could tell that the judge was very sym-
pathetic towards me – I think he fined me $100 but then he said to
them, "Would you be happy if Peter moved the barge?" and they said,
"Yeah that would solve everything." And the judge looked at me
said, "Peter, would you be happy to move the barge?" and when he
said that he winked at me. And I said, "Yeah, that's fine, I'll move
the barge." But no one, the judge included and one would think
knowingly, had specified where or how far to move it, so I moved it
a few metres and never heard anything more about it.*

It was deer farming that first led Peter to developing Mud Bay and
yet again he was involved in an industry in its early stages in New Zealand. While most Kiwis are aware of its existence, they may not realise
that deer farming originated in New Zealand and this country remains
the world's largest and most advanced in the industry. There are over 4000
deer farms in New Zealand, with approximately two million deer making
up approximately half the world's total of farmed deer.

They are not native to New Zealand, having been imported from
England and Scotland for sport in the 19th century, when they were
released mainly in the Southern Alps and its foothills in the South Island.
The environment proved to be ideal so that by the middle of the 20th
century they were regarded as pests. In the 1960s, an export market
became viable for feral deer and a few years later industry pioneers saw an
opportunity to build on this by capturing live deer and farming them. Still
relatively young the industry has expanded to the point where it is now
second only to dairy farming in terms of profitability and this, coupled
with its low labour requirements, continues to attract new farmers into
the industry.

Peter was a keen learner and his commitment increased along with
the size of his deer herds. But his decision not to settle at Mud Bay
resulted in his reluctance to further develop the property for deer farming.
Fencing and clearing paddocks was labour intensive and time consuming
and it would take many more years to increase the property's capacity to
the level he wanted. And there was still the issue of access.

He kept working and farming the property throughout the 80s and

it was an important venture for him. He was becoming ever more profi-
cient with the deer farming and was now fully committed to sustainable
forestry. He had developed the property into a viable deer farm and forestry block and in doing so had greatly enhanced its value. He needed
more space and just the next bay over was where he was looking.

Peter felt it was a good time to liquidate some of his assets and put
Mud Bay on the market. It sold quickly and at a good price. He had
recently sold Industrial Marine and he also put the *Success* on the market.
The old scow had been a solid business investment for Pete and had been
a big part of Industrial Marine's – dare one say it – success. From the Wellington Airport job to the thousands of longlines put down, it had been
a true workhorse and was also a fondly remembered pleasure boat. Rob
Pooley purchased the boat in 1990 and later on-sold it. It was ravaged by
fire in May 1995 and rather sadly was being used as a dumb barge by the
late 90s.

Kaiuma

Kaiuma Station is Peter's 2000ha property located at Kaiuma Bay, on
the north shore of the Pelorus Sound, a short boat trip (and much longer
drive) from Havelock. Peter purchased most of the current property in
1990 and many of his friends later commented that they lost sight of
Peter at that time. The previous three years had seen the share market
crash, the family feud and Peter selling Industrial Marine, which had been
such a large part of his life. It seemed now that he was living the life of
a recluse. He spent many years developing Kaiuma – clearing, planting,
bringing in stock and enlarging his deer herds.

Peter had become familiar with Kaiuma through a mate he'd gone
pig-hunting with in the area. His interest in deer farming had increased
and had been limited by the amount of usable land at Mud Bay. Shortly
before he acquired Kaiuma, he had leased some property up the Waihopai
Valley and then another property at Kaituna near Renwick to accommodate his burgeoning deer herds. The initial venture was just buying young
deer and fattening them for venison but his interest soon progressed to
breeding. Peter got a lot of good advice back then from Terrance Stirling,
who has since gone on to be a leader in the deer stud industry. Peter's

work with embryo transplants was among the first in the country and the Kaiuma farm still breeds exceptional trophy stags for game parks and the velveting market.

But when the property was on the market in 1990 it was difficult to see why anyone would want it. It is rough, hilly country running from an extensive and beautiful shoreline on the Sound up to hills 400–500m high.

> *There was the usual tangle of gorse and wattle and much of the property was on difficult terrain. Two rivers run through the property as well and needed constant attention as the area gets over 800mm of yearly rainfall. The land was partly cleared and had run a few sheep and deer. There were a few paddocks on the original property but they were in a state of neglect and not very big. I even found some dead deer in the paddocks, with no water on and it was really a case for the SPCA. So yeah, it was a bit of a mess, but it was exactly what I was looking for. I wanted to make a park that a King would want to buy.*

Pete originally leased the Kaiuma property and put a lot of effort into fencing and roadwork to make the farm usable. It soon became clear that it would make much more sense to buy the property. Ironically, the price of the property went up after he signed the lease and it seemed as if they were paying twice for some of their own efforts. The first purchase was for what is now only the farm and over the years Peter acquired adjoining waterfront land, which is now part of the Kaiuma Park Estate subdivision development.

For the first time in many years Peter was essentially working at only one thing – farming and managing the property. He cleared and prepared over 250ha to create stock paddocks for his deer herds and a sizeable mob of sheep. A lot of road building was required and Peter was again in his element on his beloved diggers and bulldozers clearing and shaping the land. He put in over 40km of road throughout the property, which was needed to bring the timber down to the water for shipping out and moving stock in and out. And while the original intent of the property was the deer farm, Peter soon became enthralled with trees. He had planted a lot of radiata at Mud Bay but now he delved into many varieties, some of which were already there in a native state but many he added. The list is long.

He put on one of the few Tasmanian Blackwood plantings in New Zealand; native matai was already there and Peter added more – in fact the flooring of the Yealands Estate Winery is matai harvested from Kaiuma Station. He added bottle brush and kowhai to attract birds, walnut, pine, macrocarpa, many varieties of gum, totara, redwood, rimu, black poplar, cherry, kahikatea, Douglas fir, red alders, willow, black cherry and oak. Many of the trees were planted in manuka groves to protect them from the prevailing winds. Chinese willows were planted as an experiment to see if the deer liked them. All the trees in the deer compounds have protective fencing around them – all planted and built by Peter. Many of the trees won't mature for another 60, 70 or 80 years so he was always taking the long view with the farm. Tens of thousands of trees were planted over time and always with an eye to conservation, sustainable forestry and attracting wildlife. There are two types of forestry at Kaiuma made up of pine and then many different varieties of natives and exotics. Whatever was farmed from the natives was limited to ten per cent of the old growth and was usually immediately replaced.

Paul Wiblin, now Pete's farm manager at Kaiuma, was living in Kaituna just outside Renwick and first met Peter in 1995. He'd gone to school with Aaron, but didn't get to know Peter until he started shearing for him at Kaiuma. In 1999 Peter was looking to move from Kaiuma because he was developing the North Bank vineyard. He was always complaining about the drive back and forth so just for a joke, Paul suggested they swap houses. Not long after Peter took him up on the idea and also asked Paul if he'd like to manage the Kaiuma farm. Paul was not really up on the deer farming business – the only experience he'd had with deer was shooting them from helicopters, he says. But he'd been travelling all over the world for ten years as a sheep-shearing contractor and was looking to settle down for a while to raise his family.

Peter put a lot of trust in Paul to run the farm as he saw fit and Paul learned about deer farming as he went. The station had already been heavily forested by Peter so the bulk of the work was keeping an eye on that, and taking care of the deer and the sheep. When Paul went out to Kaiuma there were 1000 breeding ewes, and 600 hinds and 400 velveting stags. Says Paul,

> Peter is very fair and straight up. If he asks you to do a shit job, you know that he's willing to do it himself and he's always open to your ideas, though in the end it's usually his ideas that seem to work better. And you never really know what's going to be happening – one day you'll be building a dam and the next day you'll be planting a whole hillside of trees. And he loves his big machines, I can tell you. I've seen all the moving and digging he's done at Kaiuma putting in fences, levelling paddocks, digging roads and what have you.
>
> He expects you to work as hard as he does and it's no use going to Pete and saying, "Well I've done ten hours out there now," because he'll turn around and say, "Well I've done twelve hours, mate – what are you complaining about?" But he'll say it with a smile on his face so that's okay. We've had a few rows but its funny because once it's sorted, that's it and it's like it never happened. But I can remember one time we had quite a row about some stock handling and I was pretty sure that I was right so I dug in my heels a bit on it. But he kept on and pretty much insisted that we do it his way, so we did. Anyway a couple of days later, he calls me and says, "Do you like Fiji?" Well of course I said yeah so he says, "Well you take the wife to Fiji for a week and it's on me." He didn't actually come out and say he was wrong, but I think that on second thought he reckoned that maybe I was right and that was his way of saying so. I walked around with a grin on my face for two months after that.

The station won the Marlborough Rural Environment Pastoral Award in 2003 and Paul had a lot to do with the recognition. A year before, in 2002, he'd had a field day at the farm and took a lot of tree people around to look at the trees. There was a unanimous opinion from these experts that the farm should be entered for the award. Paul remembers that the day of the judging was the same day that his wife was having a baby and, needless to say, his appearance was somewhat rushed. So winners all round. The station has also won numerous awards for its velvet.

Another one of the joys for Peter was that Aaron was spending a lot of time there working with him. "When Dad was working a lot at Kaiuma, I loved going out there. I was out every weekend helping, spraying gorse, deer velveting, there was always something to do. It was good time with Mum and Dad and at the end of the day you could look back and see what you'd accomplished. I was actually a little put out when Paul Wiblin was given the job of farm manager there – I really would've liked that, but Dad had other plans. We talked about it but Dad said I was too handy to be stuck down at the farm and we went on from there. But I was getting old enough and knew him well enough to start wondering, 'What's he going to do next?'"

Murray Mears and Larry Collins were also regulars at the farm – working, helping and sometimes just relaxing. The feral pigs were and are a constant problem so there were many good days in the bush hunting. "I did quite a bit of work at Kaiuma Station," Murray recalls, "and we ended up buying a section up there and have a house there now. We'd spend a lot of time up there when Peter and Vai had the house. We did a hell of a lot of work – clearing gorse, cutting trees and then planting new ones." Larry Collins remembers bringing in some gravel to Kaiuma.

> Pete could be a bit rough with the equipment. One day at Kaiuma I'd brought out a load of gravel in a big semi dump truck that we hadn't had too long. He was down the river building some road and he wanted me to back the truck in and spread the gravel. I wasn't too sure about it because the road was on a pretty steep slant and I told him I didn't think the truck could handle it. I said, "No no, it won't work, Peter – that's too big a slope and this thing isn't built for spreading." But he said, "Don't worry it'll be fine." Well the first load, I started putting the hoist up – he said he'd tell me when to let

the gate go and before we got the gate up, the truck promptly tipped over on its side. And Peter just stood there and laughed and laughed and I said, "What'd I bloody tell ya." I guess him laughing was his way of saying maybe, just maybe he was wrong. But sometimes you just couldn't tell him.

With the amount of work Peter was doing at Kaiuma, living in Grovetown became more and more inconvenient and so he and Vai put their lovely Mediterranean villa on the market in 1995. Pete called his real estate man and said he wanted $280k for the house, no advertising, and the agent could only bring in three prospects – and the second one bought the house. Aaron was disappointed, though he kept quiet about it. "When Dad built the stone house at Grovetown, I thought, 'This is amazing, and I'll probably inherit it.' But the old man put it on the market and it was on to something different. So I learned to not take too much for granted."

Before they shifted, an interesting thing happened. On regular drives back and forth to Blenheim, Pete and Vai used to notice a scruffy-looking paddock that was often submerged in water after a rain. When, a few years later, a For Sale sign appeared on the fence, they laughed and wondered who would be crazy enough to buy that. A couple of weeks later, Peter came home and said, "Guess what I bought?" and it was that paddock. Vai asked what he was going to do with it and Pete said he didn't know but would figure something out. It turned out that the property's former owner, wanting to save electricity, had never bothered to turn on the pumps to drain the water and the land was low and wet to start with. But Peter knew that there was fresh water flowing through it and he envisioned what could be done. He knew the area and he soon put his local knowledge to work. What he did there with his machines and the sculpting of the land is still in evidence today and aside from the picture-postcard scenery it was also Peter's first vineyard – and would soon lead to more.

With the Grovetown house sold, Peter and Vai shifted out to Kaiuma, where they would stay for five years. The farm work continued and by the end of the 90s it was indeed a park fit for a king. Pete took great pride in the property; not a gorse or thistle to be seen, thousands upon thousands of trees growing and many different birds always about. Peter had been buying up more of the shoreline on the north side of the bay and the Kaiuma Park Estate subdivision had progressed from his imagination to firm plans and into development.

The subdivision had been part of Peter's overall plans for many years but only really got going in 2005. Forty of the 215 fully-serviced sections have already been sold at prices ranging up to $300,000. The sections are either on or overlook the water and there are eventual plans for a golf course, lodge and marina. The development has also attracted the usual suspects supposedly airing their concerns of the scheme's environmental impact. Events that followed however would suggest that politics and petty animosities were also very much at play.

Part of the plans called for a causeway to shorten the drive from Havelock and to do this Pete needed a quarry. The application for resource consent was turned down the first time for safety reasons. Fair enough, thought Peter, so he acquired some adjoining land with the thought of building his own road up the hill on what was now his own property, and thought he was pretty much set to resubmit his application for the quarry. However, Peter didn't realise the depth of the opposition to the quarry or to him. A local group raised objections about it and when submissions were called for, a submission was received from this group. When hearings were held, said group was very vocal in their objections to Resource Management consent. Peter got the feeling that they didn't really have any typical "green" objections, i.e., "save the river" or that sort of thing – he felt it was more on a personal level – classic not-in-my-back-yard combined with wanting to stop Peter doing what he wanted to do. Needless to say, Peter was very annoyed and frustrated by the whole process.

In spite of these objections, Council granted the quarry resource consent with certain conditions, but the group wasn't done and filed an appeal. Peter then had to go to the Environment Court but shortly before the hearing, he received a phone call from a member of the group. This person said that because the group had spent a lot of time and money on this, if Peter came up with a specific and significant amount of cash they would withdraw the appeal.

Bad move – Pete told them to get stuffed and he'd see them in court.

If this wasn't enough, the same person then called Peter's solicitor, Miriam Radich, saying that they'd rung Peter and that Peter had refused to cooperate and repeated the cash request and could Miriam persuade Peter to go along. The court was in no position to do anything on what was legally "hearsay", though it did arrange for a very early hearing. Subsequently they had their hearing and by all accounts it was nothing short of a farce: held in small non-air-conditioned motel in Renwick in the middle of the summer, traffic noise, heat, trivial matters being discussed *ad nauseum*. Peter Radich felt that it was one of the worst examples of the RMA process he'd ever seen. Consent was finally given, and after the dust had settled it was widely thought that the complaining group's only reason for existing was to obstruct Peter's efforts.

Kaiuma Park Estate is one of the few projects Peter took on where the timing was not fortuitous and the recession in late 2008 has put it on temporary hold. Peter admits that it is a bit of a liability at present but hopes that it will be reinvigorated in the near future.

But life through the late 90s at Kaiuma was very special. Peter could see his dream becoming reality and it was a wonderful environment to live in and work in. The farm holds very warm memories for his kids. Aaron, as noted, very much enjoyed being there and would have been quite happy to settle in. Danielle, now at art school, was a regular visitor. "I always thought that the farm at Kaiuma was pretty special, but that was probably more from a kid's point of view. It was just a really neat place to go to and I have come to realise that it's quite something."

But it was that time again. Kaiuma Station was now more maintenance than development. The thinking of what could be done and the work to make it happen had been accomplished. Pete's old friend Bruce Hearn once noted, "With Peter, the thrill of the chase was better than the actual conquest. He was never a maintenance man – always an innovator and builder." And although the Kaiuma Park Estate would keep his imagination busy for a few years, the farm was, in Pete's eyes, as good as it was going to get. This mindset had already started to take hold in 1998, when he transformed that shabby wet paddock in Grovetown into his first vineyard. From here on in, it was grapes.

CHAPTER EIGHT

The Vines of Marlborough

"Drinking your first Marlborough Sauvignon Blanc is like having sex for the first time." – **Wine critic George M. Taber**

Mr Taber went on: "No other region in the world can match Marlborough, the northeastern corner of New Zealand's South Island, which seems to be the best place in the world to grow Sauvignon Blanc grapes." A bit cheeky perhaps, but testament to the worldwide enthusiasm and acceptance of Marlborough wines. It is an industry that has transformed Marlborough and other regions of New Zealand and has put the country on the international map of high-quality wines.

When Frank Yukich, son of Montana's founder, Ivan Yukich, arrived in Marlborough in 1973, all he could see was dry grass, fences, sheep and straggly trees. As he said, "Dreaming is a form of planning", which is exactly what he was doing as he looked out over the dry farmland of Marlborough. Ivan Yukich initially bought 1620ha of Marlborough farmland in 1973, in a move that seemed insane at the time but which after much soil testing, consultation and thriving vines was obviously far from crazy.

Sauvignon Blanc was not the first grape variety to be grown by Montana in Marlborough. The once-popular Müller Thurgau and some cabernets were the first grapes to be harvested and their first "sav" was planted in 1975 and harvested in 1979. The industry grew from there, slowly at first and then it caught fire in the 90s and into the 21st century. Along the way there was Montana's large-scale commercial development of vineyards in the 1970s and Hunter's Wines' success at the Sunday Times Wine Festival in 1986, frequently quoted as the event that launched Marlborough Sauvignon Blanc to the world. The other big names soon followed. Cloudy Bay Vineyards was established in 1985 and brought even more international attention to Marlborough. Although Sauvignon Blanc made up the bulk of the Marlborough product, other varieties started to make their appearance. Other whites, including pinot gris, viognier, chardonnay and riesling, are being grown and reds, notably pinot noir, are gaining a firm foothold in the region's viticulture.

As might be expected, the vineyard boom did some extraordinary things to land prices. Many farmers were only too glad to cash in and cash out, small boutique growers got involved while the prices were still somewhat sane and some landowners stayed put but switched from sheep or stone-fruit orchards to planting grapes. The growers for the most part played the spot market to sell their grapes, while some secured contracts with the larger wineries hungry for Marlborough grapes. There was no shortage of buyers, the quality of grapes was consistent throughout the region and Marlborough flourished. It was boom time and Peter was going to be a part of it.

His first vineyard was the swampy 28 hectares of paddock just north of Blenheim that Peter had purchased in 1997. When he bought it he really had no idea what he was going to do with it but grapes were starting to become a major industry in Marlborough. It took a year to prepare it and he started planting vines in 1998. This was the first vineyard in the lower Wairau valley and as usual there were the naysayers who warned Peter that the ground was too heavy and wet to sustain grapes. But Peter carried on and the vineyard is still in his possession and still producing grapes. His next vineyard was the demanding property on the North Bank of the Wairau, which he bought in 1999. A year later he bought a further two properties, one in the Riverlands area east of Blenheim and one at Mills & Ford roads, just north of Blenheim. He still owns these two and his old mate Murray Mears manages them for him, along with the original Grovetown vineyard for him.

With his purchase of a large section on the North Bank of the Wairau River, just north of Renwick, he was trying on a much more challenging project. What Peter was essentially attempting to do was build a vineyard on the stony and unwelcoming north riverbed of the Wairau. The 160ha property was a daunting venture and it was declared by all and sundry that it just wouldn't work for grapes. The property was universally derided as complete rubbish, with different and difficult elevations and covered with the ever-present gorse that tangled and tore at anything and anybody that ventured onto it.

The property had belonged to Richard and Simon Adams, the same Adams family whose non-feral goats had got Pete and Murray into trouble many years before. The Adams family were also clients of Peter's accountant, Steven Startup, who knew that the property was sitting there doing nothing. Steven started talking to Peter about developing the area as a vineyard and secured a peppercorn lease for it. The project was largely based on Steven's initiative and would attest to his good business sense that cheap land plus Peter Yealands made a good combination. Prior to doing any development, Peter bought one of the neighbouring properties. It was covered in old pine trees that were slowly dying so Peter cleared it out and developed it as a base to work from. Shortly thereafter he purchased the property outright and got on with the North Bank development. He got stuck in and worked at this and nothing else for two years.

It was at this time that he yet again shifted the family residence. He tried the drive back and forth from Kaiuma for a month or two but knew that it just wasn't going to work and that was when he and Paul Wiblin swapped houses. It also marked the end of Peter's focus on Kaiuma. While he still owned the farm and has subsequently started work on the subdivision development there, he was caught up in the vineyard and in his big machines, sculpting new land. Within eighteen months, the North Bank was turned into a thriving and beautifully landscaped vineyard.

As it turned out, and perhaps serendipitously, the job as Peter had it in mind was never finished. In 2001 a friend in the real estate business asked to see the vineyards and Peter was glad to show him around. A few weeks later the same estate agent asked if he could show the property to some visiting Australians and Peter said go ahead. Another few weeks went by and the agent asked Peter if he was interested in selling the property, but Peter was cool to the idea. As far as he was concerned, he wasn't finished and wanted to keep on with it. He had big plans for the property and wanted to build a park-like setting for the vineyard. His plans included a restaurant and wetlands park with live crayfish and pots so punters could pull their own freshwater lobsters out of the pond. He had spoonbills coming in to nest and had always loved planting native trees to entice the birds. He'd had truckloads of dried mussel shells brought down from Havelock, resulting in gleaming white roads throughout the property. But the agent said he reckoned he could sell it and started talking big dollars, which Peter quickly translated into a very tidy $7 million profit. And Peter got to thinking about what he could do with that.

Peter has always had an ambivalent attitude to money. He has never coveted it nor had dreams of being a rich man, but money has its place. To Pete, money is another tool; it's a big paper bulldozer that can make things happen. It turned out that the Australians who had visited the property were from the brewing giant Fosters, and shortly thereafter they made Peter an offer that he couldn't refuse. The property was sold for upwards of $14 million and the profit enabled Peter to start thinking about the next big thing. He'd already been out to see some farms at Seaview, just east of Seddon, and had started thinking about its potential. Peter was going to build the largest privately owned vineyard in New Zealand.

Seaview

The first thing you notice as you drive east on Seaview Road from Seddon, which is 25km south of Blenheim, is that you're not on the Wairau plains anymore. Once over the Dashwood Pass and into the Awatere River valley the landscape and climate change dramatically. It is rough, tussocky country and you wonder how people ever made a living out there. As the road heads ever eastward, the Cook Strait comes into view and on clear days the North Island looks close enough to swim to. The land is rolling and looks down on the Awatere River, which hems it in to the north. The wind seems to be constantly blowing, either the baking Marlborough nor'wester or a bitter south-easterly off the ocean. What you see now is what Peter alone saw in his mind's eye in 2001.

Seddon is not big; its population in 2001 was only 477 and indicated a disturbing decrease of 69 souls since 1996. Not surprising when you look at the land. Peter paid a reported $12000 a hectare for the farms and budgeted a comparable amount to develop the land. He has been welcomed to the area and not just because he arrived with deep pockets;

his hard-working, practical background is the sort of thing Seddon folk like. As one local put it, he's not just respected for his business nous and the jobs he's created, he's truly liked. When Peter finished his buying, he had laid claim to 1000ha of some of the roughest terrain in the region. Along with the property he obtained crucial water rights and immediately started designing and building a sophisticated irrigation system to bring water up from the Awatere. Once again, it was time to get to work and the key word throughout this development would be sustainability.

Peter noted in his Thrive Wellington speech that over the years he had pounded in a million fence posts and planted over two million vines. The bulk of these went into the Seaview vineyard. The irrigation system is a marvel to all who see it and visitors often ask which company put it in only to be told that Peter put it in himself. He was at the forefront of using GPS technology to accurately map the terrain and guide the earth-moving equipment and it is the extent to which the land has been sculpted that is the real story of the Seaview vineyard.

The vineyard is a model of terrace design, which is a relatively new technique in vineyard development. Where there were constant rough ups and downs, there are now gentle undulations. Sharp hilltops have vanished and the earth moved into lower areas, providing a much easier terrain to plant and work on. The GPS helped identify not just the flow of the land which would allow for the run-off and flow of water; it also made it possible to structure a terrain that took the air-flow into consideration to provide additional protection from frost. Peter also insisted upon wetlands and over twenty have been incorporated into the vineyard and they attract many species of birds. When those first young vines were planted, Peter invented a now-patented protection device to shield the fledgling vines. And, to no one's surprise, another very important component was the trees. In many vineyards trees are often the first victims of development, but at Seaview it is just the opposite. He has planted thousands of trees – some to complement the wetland areas and others lining the roads into and throughout the vineyard. Within six years he had done it: Seaview was the largest privately-owned vineyard in New Zealand and an industry standard of sustainable viticulture.

Pete and Vai took up residence there in 2002 – where they still live

– in a modest farm house that came with one of the farms. Accommodation and facilities were put in for the workers and a large machine and equipment complex was built which son Aaron now manages. Living on site has always been Peter's preference, but looking back he admits to missing Kaiuma.

> *I loved it out there, though it's now really a shadow of what it was. It would have been nice perhaps to retire there, but Vai wasn't really interested in that and of course in the meantime other things have come along. I'm only out there three, four times a year now and it just gets me down. It was a full-time job for me for almost ten years and I loved the work and the planting. It was immaculate and a real showcase, with thousands of trees planted – both natives and some rare exotics that are probably not seen anywhere else in the South Island. So the whole thing is for sale – though in the current market there won't be many punters so I could be with Kaiuma for a while yet. When I was down there, I was actually skinny – didn't have this big gut I've got now from sitting at my desk. I was as fit as and really loved the life out there.*

Peter's next job was selling grapes and he would depend initially, like many, on the spot market. This worked well when the prices were high and every grape had a value but Pete had enough experience to know that it probably couldn't last and he was thinking about the next move. His inclination toward acquisition was also showing itself and he became interested in a company called Oyster Bay Marlborough Vineyards.

CHAPTER NINE

The Grapes of Math at Oyster Bay

"The best business story of 2005." – **David W. Young,** *New Zealand Listener*

eter was always looking for investment and acquisition opportunities and he and his accountant Stephen Startup would often drive around Marlborough looking at properties. This was how he first became aware of Oyster Bay: 500 prime hectares of vineyard and already boasting one of the iconic New Zealand wine brands. Oyster Bay had been owned by Delegat's Wine Estate Limited and was incorporated in 1999, with Delegat's Wine Estate Limited as a principal shareholder. There were five directors on the board of Oyster Bay, two from Delegat's and three independent directors who were major New Zealand business and government figures. Bill Falconer, former stock-exchange market surveillance panel chairman; Ruth Richardson, former National Government Finance Minister; and John Maasland, previous CEO of Wilson & Horton Group. (In 2005, Maasland was replaced by Ross Keenan, a professional director.) After incorporation Oyster Bay offered 9 million shares at $2.00 per share to the public and Delegat's undertook to retain at least 20 per cent of the shares in Oyster Bay for at least five years.

Noted economist and business commentator Brian Gaynor's 2005 article includes a comprehensive and trenchant analysis of the float:

Pulling the cork on wine takeover issues

…In his letter to investors [Oyster Bay director Bill] Falconer wrote: "Delegat's Wine Estate Ltd has made a significant financial commitment to the future of Oyster Bay by agreeing to subscribe for a minimum of 20 per cent of Oyster Bay's share capital".

According to the offer document the $18 million raised would be used as follows:

$5.9 million to purchase the Gifford's Creek vineyard from Delegat's.

$4.2 million to buy the Airfields vineyard from Delegat's.

An additional $4.2 million to develop the Airfields vineyard.

Further capital expenditure of $2.2 million.

Working capital provision and offer expenses of $1.5 million.

…The Oyster Bay share issue was an incredibly sweet deal for Delegat's. The promoter committed to outlay only $3.6 million for its minimum 20 per cent stake yet it was selling two vineyards for $10.1 million and transferring significant development costs to the new company. In addition, Delegat's retained the management contract over the two vineyards and has veto powers over the sale of the properties to an outside party until June 2049…

Oyster Bay joined the NZAX, the alternative market share market, when it opened in November 2003. At that stage the vineyard owner had completed five full years and had only exceeded its prospectus net surplus forecast in two of the five years. The company should probably not have been allowed to list on the NZX because its relationship with Delegat's was far too close and requires waivers from the exchange's important related party transaction rules. On NZAX listing, Delegat's Wine Estate owned 32.6 per cent of Oyster Bay compared with 29.8 per cent a year earlier. It is unclear why Delegat's was not subject to the requirements of the Takeovers Code when it raised its shareholding from 29.8 per cent to 32.6 per cent…"[5]

---

5. New Zealand Herald, 9 October 2005. Reprinted with kind permission from Brian Gaynor.

The 1999 prospectus was quite clear about Oyster Bay's exclusive agreement with Delegat's Wine Estate: "Delegat's has contracted with Oyster Bay to purchase all grapes produced by the vineyards at market price for a minimum of twenty years."[6]

Peter was interested in investing in the initial float but Startup felt that it wasn't as rosy as depicted and advised Peter not to invest at that time. Peter took Stephen's advice, though Oyster Bay's seemingly unbound potential for both the production of grapes and as a profitable investment would remain in his mind.

Meanwhile he tended to his many other business enterprises, but kept a close eye on Oyster Bay. Startup's advice proved to be prescient because to Peter's bewilderment the company's shares were consistently poor performers. In 2003 he was still intrigued with Oyster Bay and, reckoning that it should be a money-maker, he started to buy shares in the company. But nothing had changed: the returns on shares were still drastically lower than anticipated, with the share price mired in the low $2 range for one of the best vineyards in Marlborough. He started to ask himself why this undeniably premium location and brand was showing such poor returns. He looked closer and the arithmatic seemed pretty simple. Taking into consideration the normal costs of operating a vineyard of that size, its output, and the assumed market price being paid by Delegat's Group Ltd (DGL), the maths indicated that the company should be very profitable. He reckoned that there were only two possible reasons for the poor share performance: Management – Oyster Bay itself had no employees and was being managed by Delegat's so it was possible that costs being charged by DGL to Oyster Bay were too high and/or the management was below standard. Or…the price that Oyster Bay was getting for its grapes was too low, though this was contrary to what was stated in the original prospectus.

Peter wasn't ready to believe the second reason so he focused on the first. He believed he had enough experience in the vineyard business to turn Oyster Bay around and his interest in the company now evolved from a straight investment opportunity to a management and ownership

---

6. Signed by Jim Delegat, OBMV 1999 Prospectus.

opportunity. And so Peter Yealands started contemplating the takeover of Oyster Bay.

It would not be easy as DGL was the majority shareholder, with approximately 33 percent ownership, and many of the smaller shareholders were probably inclined to be loyal to Jim Delegat. As Peter got into it, it became apparent there was more to it than met the eye. As a shareholder in Oyster Bay he started asking questions of the directors, as it was plain to see that either costs were too high or prices were too low, but the information was not forthcoming. And while it was known that Oyster Bay had an exclusive contract with the Delegat's Group for the purchase of their grapes, neither Oyster Bay nor DGL was willing to divulge pricing information to the minority shareholders. Peter's share volume had now reached 5 percent, which at this point became public knowledge, and as his ownership increased he would have to publicly state his intentions. His intentions were now firmly leaning toward an attempted takeover of Oyster Bay and with that in mind he approached his Marlborough lawyers, Radich Dwyer.

The team was also joined by high-flying New Zealand businessman Bruce Hancox. Bruce had been a major player in New Zealand business, with over thirty-five years of corporate experience in manufacturing and retailing. This experience notably included nineteen years with Brierley Investments Limited, where he served as Group Chief Executive Officer and Chairman of the Board, during which time the market capitalisation of that company increased from NZ$28 million to NZ$7 billion. He was a tough, knowledgeable money-man and Peter Radich had the feeling that Bruce and Peter Yealands would get along. He also knew that if Bruce was interested he would be able to provide valuable advice and assistance in the takeover bid. After their initial 2004 meeting in Nelson it was apparent that Yealands and Hancox saw eye to eye on a lot of things. Bruce knew a lot about the rough and tumble world of corporate takeovers, mergers and acquisitions and had been the driving force behind the merger of three brands that now operate under the Corbans name. Considering his previous experience he felt that he could make a significant contribution to the effort and decided to get involved.

Already holding 6.71 per cent of Oyster Bay shares, Peter initiated a partial takeover bid on 4 June 2005, for 51.1 percent of the shares with an initial offer price of $3.10. DGL quickly responded with a competing offer and the bidding war began, quickly reaching $4.00. All the while DGL had also been purchasing shares and in August they reached 50.1 per cent. It seemed as if the story was over and the takeover bid done and dusted. But at that point, Peter and another minority shareholder, David Rankin, raised serious questions about the company valuations as stated in the initial Target Company Statement (TCS) and DGL's grape pricing with Oyster Bay. Consequently they made official complaints to the Takeover Panel regarding both issues. What transpired resulted in a precedent-setting legal decision that saw the first ever reversal of a corporate takeover in New Zealand. It was well summed up in the following blog entry:

Bad for business – 6 December 2005, by frog

It is common coin in current economic commentary that New Zealanders invest too much money in property and not enough in the share market. Well, last week a story that's been brewing for six months finally ripened to a point that may help commentators understand why. Namely, the shenanigans at Oyster Bay Marlborough Vineyards (OBMV)…

According to their website, OBMV has one customer, Delegat's wines, who has a 20-year contract to buy OBMV grapes at market rates. Considering how the company was formed this is not a surprise. Things got a tiny bit more interesting in May. OBMV received notice of a takeover offer from Peter Yealands who wanted to buy four million shares, which would mean that he would end up owning 51 percent of OBMV. Unless you owned shares in OBMV, why should you care? The frog does not, and the frog did not.

Peter Y was offering $3.10 a share in May 2005. In June Delegat's made a counter offer at $3.20 a share. Over the next month or so both bidders raised their offers to $4. On 9 August Delegat's announced it had won.

But all is not as it seems. When the bidding war started

the independent directors sent a report to the shareholders of Oyster Bay which valued the company at $45m. Yet according to the *Dominion Post* and *The Independent* (16 November) there was a valuation of $51m a week before. Then the following caught the frog's attention. In a lead story, *The Independent* (30 November) reported from the High Court: The Problem: Christine Pears, who is both Oyster Bay's company secretary and Delegat's chief financial officer, signed the TCS (Target Company Statement). The document went out to shareholders with a $45 million valuation of Oyster Bay's vineyards but Pears knew a more up-to-date valuation of $51 million had been done. Her failure to disclose it was due to "inadvertence" and "her limited role in the takeover process," Delegat's told the court.

…The case also opened up other nagging doubts for shareholders. Of particular concern is Mr. Yealands' persistent complaint, backed by affidavits referred to by Justice Miller, [alleging] that Delegat's has been paying below-market value for its grapes. But remember, OBMV… says that Delegat's pays market price for its grapes.

So what should a small shareholder in OBMV think of this? The major shareholder is getting a good deal. Major shareholder then tries to take over the company (and become a majority share holder) on the back of too-low valuations. The independent directors not only signed off those valuations but allowed the major shareholder to [allegedly] buy grapes cheap. The independent directors negotiate the price… in negotiations kept secret from shareholders. On the reported evidence, one could question whether the independent directors were working for all the shareholders or not.

The people mostly responsible for this mess, those independent directors Bill Falconer, Ruth Richardson and Ross Keenan, are pillars of the New Zealand business community, the same community that lambasts the Greens for being bad for business. [7]

Also of interest are some items in the summations by Justice Miller, who presided over the case in the High Court:

High Court Wellington, 7 October 2005, Miller, J.
{54}...There is force in the evidence of Greg Antony Anderson, an economist engaged by Mr Rankin, that the discrepancy suggests either that the DCF [valuation] model used to assess the encumbered land value has been applied incorrectly or that Delegat's is paying a below-market price for grapes... [8]

High Court of New Zealand – Wellington Registry, 28 November 2005, Miller, J.
{18}...A Marlborough winemaker, Matthew John Thomson, has sworn an affidavit in which he expresses the opinion that Oyster Bay should have enjoyed a premium of $200 per tonne over district average prices for sauvignon blanc and $500 per tonne for chardonnay varieties. He has also examined the prices that Oyster Bay was paid in the 2004 and 2005 years and concluded that it actually received less than the district averages. The [alleged] difference between the prices received and market prices for premium grapes, based on volume of grapes produced, was $1,455,358.60 in 2004 and $1,115,154.83 in 2005... [9]

The business media was now taking notice of this "bearded Swanndri-wearing bloke". David W. Young labelled it the business story of 2005 and noted: "...The case went to the High Court, which made legal history by backing the [Takeover] panel and canning the Delegat offer. The court agreed that the Oyster Bay directors had provided unsound information.

---

7. Reprinted with kind permission from 'frogblog', at http://blog.greens.org.nz/
8. CIV 2005-485-2047, CIV 2005-485-2058.
9. CIV 2005-485-2058.

Those directors unexpectedly end 2005 with red faces."[10]

Though Peter had been somewhat vindicated by the Takeover Panel's decision, it had been a rough year for him. In the national media coverage of the events he was often portrayed as the naïve interloper meddling in things he knew little about, and as a burr under the saddle of the New Zealand wine establishment. The two men had appeared on national television; Jim Delegat, well-dressed and media-savvy on one side, and Peter Yealands, visibly uncomfortable and somewhat scruffy on the other. And so the takeover battle resumed.

Round 2

Peter Yealands had already committed himself to a $4.50 share price offer and again the bidding was started. With bids and counterbids it didn't take long for the price to approach $6.00 but the cost of a successful takeover was fast becoming problematic. There was also the stark reality that Delegat's only needed 18 per cent to reach 51 per cent, while Yealands needed 44 per cent, and that Delegat's would probably reach that total sooner. Then, in December 2005, at the behest of DGL, the two parties met and came to an agreement that ended Peter's battle for the takeover of Oyster Bay. But if Peter thought that Oyster Bay's business would improve or that DGL were ready to buy his outstanding shares, he would be disappointed on both counts.

His next step was to file a civil claim with the High Court alleging that since his participation as a shareholder from 2004 to the present, Oyster Bay was being operated to the prejudice of its minority shareholders and to the benefit of its major shareholder (DGL) on the basis of unfair grape prices. This claim started its inexorable languid progress through the legal system, and Peter got on with other business. He was thinking about building a winery.

In February 2008, NZPA filed the following report: "Oyster Bay Marlborough Vineyards (OBMV) today reported its December half year net loss widened to $707,000 from $299,000 a year earlier... Chairman Bill Falconer said... legal disputes with Peter Yealands Investment Ltd

---

10. The *New Zealand Listener*, 24 December 2005.

(PYIL) over costs associated with the takeover actions in 2006 remained unresolved…"[11] Oyster Bay MV might be wallowing in red figures but it was a banner year for Delegat's. They were awarded the Deloitte/Management Magazine Company of the Year award for their "outstanding market performance and growth, underpinned by a world-class product and stand-out consumer branding."Their 2008 Annual Report, riding the success of the Oyster Bay brand, boasted the following results:

> Achieved record global sales of 1,449,000 cases.
> Achieved record total revenue of $165.3 million.
> Achieved record net profit of $19.1 million.
> Led the New Zealand wine industry with the Oyster Bay
> brand being the number one selling New Zealand wine brand
> in the United Kingdom, Australia and Canada.

In 2009 Delegat's carried on with yet more record numbers: $229.4 million total revenue and net profit after tax of $30.0 million. While at Oyster Bay, the 2009 Annual Report showed revenue down to $3.97 million, though it must be said that the profit "improved" to a loss of $599,000.

The inherent dichotomy of the situation was not lost on veteran business reporter Allan Swann, who had followed this story from the start.

> Adding spice to the ongoing court drama has been accusa-
> tions by Yealands and other critics that OBMV (Oyster Bay)
> may be selling its grapes at below market rates to Delegat's,
> helping boost that company's numbers. Given that Delegat's
> is OBMV's major shareholder, it has been suggested that
> Delegat's has effectively been shuffling dividends to its books
> – at the expense of OBMV's minority shareholders. Delegat's
> Group's profits have bubbled over with the winemaker report-
> ing half year net profit fizzing up 146 percent to $15.7 million
> back in February, while OBMV reported a loss of $830,000

---

11. *National Business Review* online, 27 February 2008.

in the same six months, blaming interest rate hedges and tax adjustments. It doesn't help that Jim Delegat and Rob Wilton sit on both company boards. These accusations have been refuted by both the NZX, as market regulator, and the company's independent directors. [12]

Looking at the chronically poor share price of the publicly traded Oyster Bay Marlborough Vineyards as opposed to the consistently profitable results of the Oyster Bay brand, it's easy to believe that something wasn't right. Sadly for investors and shareholders, the share price was based not on the value of the company but on the profitability of the company. And since its inception, Oyster Bay Marlborough Vineyards had never been a significantly profitable company.

Compare this with a statement that Jim Delegat made in August 2008: "We just want to see Oyster Bay achieve what it set out to do. That was to be a vineyard investment for the investing public, which we would manage and buy the grapes at annually negotiated prices." [13] And in the same article: "Peter Yealands established a crusade claiming to represent minority interests. Our view is that he's destroyed significant shareholder value over the last two years. What he's really trying to do is leverage his position so Delegat's has to buy his minority shareholding out. He is promoting self interest and is a very unpopular figure at AGM meeting time."

The legal proceedings dragged on through 2009. A trial date was finally set for August 2010 but as expected an out-of-court settlement was reached and on 1 July 2010 the Delegat's Group Ltd released the following statement:

> Delegat's Group will increase its holding in Oyster Bay
> Marlborough Vineyards to 54.92 per cent under a settle-
> ment of long-running legal proceedings with Peter Yealands
> and Peter Yealands Investments. The proceedings arose from
> a five-month battle for control between Oyster Bay's main
> shareholders, Delegat's and Yealands, in 2005. Delegat's will

---

12. *NBR* online, 19 June 2009.

13. *NBR* article by Allan Swann, 28 August 2008.

buy all of Yealands' 433,816 shares in Oyster Bay, equal to 4.82 per cent of the company, at $1.80 a share. Delegat's will pay an allowance towards costs of $200,000 to Yealands to settle the proceedings and Yealands will pay $150,000 plus GST to Oyster Bay to settle takeover costs. Settlement is on July 31, 2010. Oyster Bay chairman Sandy Maier said that in view of the costs and business disruption involved in prosecuting and defending the various claims, the terms of the settlement were commercially and financially compelling. Jim Delegat, the managing director of Delegat's, said the settlement was in the best interests of the shareholders of both companies.[14]

Along with the poor share price, this agreement also included the legal constraints that are noted at the end of this chapter. The published statement seems to disclose all the financial aspects of the share purchase and the settlement of associated costs, so the confidentiality restraints add further fuel to the speculation that there was still something to hide.

Sour Grapes

Since then, the recession, combined with the grape glut, started taking its toll. As in any stressed economic climate, companies with foresight, good management and sound financial foundations usually ride out the storm while those without falter. Oyster Bay Marlborough Vineyards was past faltering; it was floundering.

In the *New Zealand Herald* of 16 April 2010, Owen Hembry wrote, "Warnings of losses and broken bank covenants by Oyster Bay Marlborough Vineyards reflect the challenges facing the wine industry, say observers." Hembry wrote again in the *Herald* on 9 June 2010: "Listed grape grower Oyster Bay Marlborough Vineyards is reviewing its capital structure after two years of lower grape prices, says chairman Sandy Maier…total revenue received was down 28 per cent on the previous year at $8.3 million, resulting in a forecast end-of-year operating loss after tax of about $900,000 before adjustment."

---

14. NZPA, 1 July 2010.

But a saviour arrived and in the *Herald* on 19 October 2010 Hembry wrote, "Delegat's Group is making a takeover bid for grape grower Oyster Bay, which it says has been hit by an oversupply of wine and price pressure. NZX-listed Delegat's has offered $1.80 a share in a full takeover of NZAX-listed Oyster Bay Marlborough Vineyards, which values the company at $16.2 million. Oyster Bay's grape sales for the year ending June 30 were down 28 per cent at $8.3 million, with an operating loss of $841,000." Perhaps looking for a good deal and a large rug to sweep everything under, the Delegat Group completed the total buy-out and re-privatisation of Oyster Bay in December 2010.

Jim Delegat was twice invited to provide comments for this book. In August 2010, his office was contacted and Delegat personally replied, declining to comment. The author also spoke with him in April 2009 and Delegat's reply was, "Why would I want to contribute anything to Peter Yealands. He's a man of limited intelligence and irrational thinking, and I think if you continue to hold off and watch this space, you will see a lot of things unfold."

And indeed a lot of things did unfold. Through myriad actions and inactions, Oyster Bay has been a solid loser from the get-go. In 2010 their share price dipped as low as $1.40 and in late 2010 was languishing at $1.85. The OBMV 2010 Annual Report noted the following: "The Company's audited financial performance for 2010 is a net loss after tax of $13,820,000 compared with a net profit after tax of $1,538,000 in the previous year."

Looking back

To be sure, there may be some legitimate reasons for OBMV's poor performance: perhaps an oversupply of grapes in the later years and/or legal costs were a drag on resources. But looking at the whole story of Oyster Bay, including the Siamese-twin-like closeness of the companies, the stellar share performance of Delegat's vs the mediocre performance of Oyster Bay Marlborough Vineyards despite the international success of the Oyster Bay brand, and both companies' secretiveness about the pricing negotiations, there seems to be good reason to suspect that Delegat's did not pay market prices for Oyster Bay's grapes.

What many have taken away from the Oyster Bay saga is that Jim Delegat was in error thinking that Peter Yealands would bow to his polished, pin-striped pressure and back off. Contrary to many opinions at the time that Peter didn't know with whom he was tangling, it could just as easily be said that Jim Delegat didn't know with whom *he* was tangling. Time and time again we've seen that the most consistent characteristic of Peter Yealands is that he never gives up. Also evident is some very poor character judgement on Delegat's part. To label Peter Yealands a man of "limited intelligence and irrational thinking" is laughable for those who know Peter and bad news for those who take that judgement to heart.

To be fair, one has to accept the fact that Jim Delegat could see that Peter Yealands was a potential competitor and a tough one at that. And it is true that when the takeover battle was done, Peter's shares were at a higher price than when he purchased them (though not by the time he was finally bought out). And whatever else was going on, Peter was rocking a big boat in a big way and one can understand Delegat's apprehension and animosity.

There were two key issues running through this story. First there was the refusal of the minority shareholders' requests for access to the same information that the majority shareholder had. To some minority shareholders this seemed unethical, and even if DGL and Oyster Bay were within their rights to withhold the pricing information some investors were left wondering what they had to hide.

Secondly, how fair, ethical, and perhaps even legal were the secret business practices between the Delegat's Group and Oyster Bay Marlborough Vineyards – practices which seem to have doomed Oyster Bay first to fiscal mediocrity and then fiscal oblivion?

Oyster Bay was significantly funded by public punters who have to rely on what they read in a company's prospectus. They also have to trust respected business leaders to act in a decent and ethical manner. Oyster Bay's punters could be forgiven for wondering whether their faith had been misplaced.

Author's statement

As of 1 July 2010, Peter Yealands and his advisors have agreed as part of a settlement to refrain from publicly discussing any of the matters concerning Oyster Bay Marlborough Vineyards, the Delegat's Group (DGL) and the Oyster Bay takeover attempt in 2005. It should be noted that this book was not commissioned by Peter Yealands or any of his advisors and that the writing and publication was at the instigation of the author. It must also be noted that any comments made to the author by Peter Yealands and/or his advisors concerning Oyster Bay and/or the Delegat's Group Ltd were made prior to 1 July 2010.

The Oyster Bay takeover bid was well-publicised. Much of the information in this chapter was gleaned from the media and from comments and opinions provided by other interested observers and independent sources. It includes the opinions of the author and others, which do not necessarily represent those of Peter Yealands, his advisors or the publisher.

CHAPTER TEN

Yealands Estate Winery

The most environmentally pioneering winery in the world

– Great Wine Capitals, 2010

Yealands Estate Winery is the future. The twin goals of producing good wine and doing so in a sustainable and energy efficient manner have been realised by the visionary efforts of Peter Yealands and his team. It is the logical progression on the path that Peter embarked on when he developed the vineyard. In his previous vineyards and with the Sea-view vineyard at its inception, Peter depended upon the spot market for selling his grapes and from the late 90s through to 2006 that was satisfactory. The market was strong and as we have seen there was no shortage of wineries vying to obtain Marlborough grapes. But three things were apparent to Peter. First, the size of the new vineyard meant that he was now harvesting a huge amount of grapes and to be dependent on outside buyers was a potentially precarious business position to be in. Second, there was no guarantee that grape prices would remain at a high level or that the demand for Marlborough grapes would always exceed the supply. And most importantly, the concept of the complete enterprise – from the vineyard to the consumer – strongly appealed to his innate insistence on seeing a job through to its completion. So in early 2006 Peter began planning the Yealands Estate Winery.

The winery is now the jewel and central focus of his 1000ha viticultural enterprise on Seaview Road, 5km east of Seddon in the Awatere Valley. As you drive out over the rolling hills, with stunning glimpses of the North Island as a backdrop to the thousands of meticulous rows of vines, you start to appreciate the huge efforts that were necessary to make this happen. There is still no winery in sight until you go over the top of the last hill and then the full magnitude of the facility spreads before you. The sweeping curves of each of the twin building modules in mirror image to each other fit in so well to the surrounding environment that at first you don't realise how big it is. But as you get closer and drive around to the front entrance you realise that this is not your average winery.

Stepping inside, your eyes are drawn to the glowing wood of the reception area and the natural warmth of the matai floors, all milled from Peter's sustainable native forests at Kaiuma. Walk through to the spacious Cellar Door and you encounter the natural look of stone and matai and the many eye-catching works of art adorning the walls. Adjoining the space is a separate audio-visual theatre where visitors can watch the story of this ground-breaking endeavour on the big video screen.

Go into the winemaking facility and the size and scope of the enterprise really hits home – this is a big place. When the winery opened in August 2008 only one side of the building was in production, with the winery processing approximately 5000 tonnes, but as each stage was completed over the next three years the capacity expanded to its projected level of 11,000 tonnes. Under the sweeping curve of the roof soaring overhead, the sparkling stainless steel tanks tower over you and the cleanliness and methodical order of everything is immediately apparent.

Walk through to the back of the building and outside is a vast array of structures: loading ramps, walkways, conveyors, stainless steel bins and electronic monitoring panels controlling the influx of grapes from the vineyards. The two wind turbines are precursors to the comprehensive sustainable energy production planned for the complex. Overall is the look of leading-edge technology, efficiency and spotless attention to detail. Being green is one thing; to be so in a productive and professional operation of this magnitude is a testament to the enterprise's dedication to practical sustainability.

In the beginning

As part of the planning, Peter was advised to bring together an advisory group to help guide him through the project. Unlike a corporate board of directors their sole function would be to advise and to make available their specific areas of expertise. However, like any major board of directors, they are prominent figures in New Zealand business, giving an indication of the respect that Peter engenders.

Long-time friend, one-time neighbour and eminent lawyer, Peter Radich, was the architect of Pete's advisory group for the Yealands Estate Winery. At the time of writing he is District Solicitor for Marlborough District, Chairman of the Broadcast Standards Authority and Milk Commissioner for the Fonterra Group responsible for dispute resolution between Fonterra and its shareholders. He is also a former Vice President of the New Zealand Law Society and was Marlborough District coroner for twenty-seven years. Over the years Radich had come to know Peter well and the two men have a strong and mutual respect for each other.

Radich knew winemaker Matt Thomson and held him in high regard. He approached Matt with the idea of joining the board and Matt agreed to this. Matt is a well-respected winemaker and consultant with notable successes both locally and internationally over a variety of wine styles, with particular strengths in Marlborough's iconic Sauvignon Blanc. He has been involved with five separate winery design and build projects and also spends considerable time in the international market place speaking and promoting the interests of both clients and the greater New Zealand wine industry. Matt is also co-owner and winemaker for Delta Wines and won the highly coveted White Wine Maker of the Year at the 2008 International Wine Challenge awards in London.

It was also agreed that Yealands Estate required some high-level financial advice and guidance. Radich approached John Waller, who at that time was a senior partner of Price Waterhouse Coopers in Auckland. John Waller is also chairman of the Bank of New Zealand and is on the board of directors for Fonterra. One of the top financial advisors in the country, he operated at the highest levels of corporate finance, but he was someone whom Radich thought would be able to identify with Peter. John's reputation is such that he is continuously being asked to help in various projects but time and interest constraints usually resulted in his turning down such requests. Much to both Peters' credit he said yes and became an important part of the group.

Pete now had a formidable brains trust put together and although

Matt Thomson left the group once the wine-making process was fully operational, Peter Radich and John Waller have stayed on and are trusted advisors in the on-going management of the business.

Now Peter could get on with building a winery.

When I started thinking about wineries, I spoke with my old mate Graeme Giles, whose wife Annie is Annie's Foods, just north of Blenheim. Graeme showed me around his new factory that had just been built by Apollo Projects of Christchurch. Graeme has always been keen about saving energy and had remarked about the great job that Apollo had done. Anyway I got together with Paul Lloyd of Apollo and we got started. I then started thinking about the actual design and being a bit of an environmentalist, I wanted something that was going to be aesthetically pleasing to the eye and minimise its impact on its natural surroundings. The first thing you notice out here is the rolling hills and that essentially is where the basic design came from. I had seen a similar design in America which I quite liked, and although the methodology used there was not going to work here, the low, rounded curves of the buildings stayed with me.

Apollo Projects Ltd of Christchurch had a lot of experience in the wine industry and was keen to enable Peter's vision to become a reality. They had been involved in winery projects in Central Otago and Marlborough and were able to draw on their experience throughout all aspects of the Yealands Estate Winery project. Apollo is also firmly committed to sustainability, furthering the strength and compatibility of the relationship with Peter. Although the company has worked on various types of projects, they consider the wine industry to be their core business. With particular expertise in controlled environment projects, it was a good fit all round.

Paul Lloyd, CEO and founder of the company, is responsible for the overall management of Apollo and also has a key role as a project director on major projects, managing the design process, establishing the structure of a project and carrying through with client and financial reporting and relationship management. Paul remembers the start of the project.

We heard rumours that this guy who owned a big vineyard up there was planning to build a winery so in June 2006 we called him up. Peter's reputation had preceded him and we weren't too sure whether he'd be interested in seeing us, but he was and we got together. So there we were in the kitchen of his little farmhouse with tea and biscuits and over the next little while a bond developed which carried on from there right through to completion of the project. He liked that we weren't one of the many big companies that had been knocking on his door. What was really interesting was that when we first talked, he didn't have a brand, didn't have a winery – he just had this idea about building a world-class winery. He really became the perfect client because we pride ourselves on our ability to help develop ideas like this and he was very open and receptive to our input. This is not to say that he didn't have firm ideas of his own because he certainly did, but he also realised that he needed help to make this all happen and it turned into a very reward-ing and productive relationship.

Peter was aware that entering into a global market needed more than just a brand and a product. He knew that he needed something different that would set him apart from the rest of the competition. He was already keenly aware of the importance of sustainability and with Apollo's similar ideology, the whole concept of an absolute commitment to sustainability was quickly and mutually agreed upon as a major key to the venture's suc-cess and future. This concept proved to be a motivation to both Apollo and Peter to see just how far they could take it and as it fitted into both parties' philosophy, the project quickly gained traction. Aside from all the "feel-good" aspects of the project, in the end all decisions were solidly based on good business. Apollo provided cost-benefit analyses through-out to confirm the business viability of every aspect of the project to determine what made sense and what didn't. And while Peter had always thought positively about sustainability, the actual scope of the opportunity was one that grew and grew as the project proceeded.

The Build

The site was settled on in September 2006 and once the go-ahead for starting was obtained in March 2007, the actual construction of the facility began that May. The budget was $45–50 million and the job was completed on time and on budget for the opening in August 2008. Costs were approximately $22 million for the building itself with another $20 million allocated for the wine-making plant equipment. Landscaping – a lot of it done by Peter himself – added to the final tally.

Robinson Construction Ltd of Blenheim was one of the main contractors for the project and Nick Robinson recalls the construction of the building.

> We had worked with Apollo Projects before on other wineries and had developed a very good relationship with them. The actual building of the winery presented very few problems, though working to the Green standards was relatively new to us. For the most part, it was a matter of carefully monitoring our recycling and sourcing as much as we could locally. The site manager would continually monitor our efforts and keep us on track as far as that went, so although it was a bit of a learning curve for us, it didn't really present any problems. It's interesting that these new Green standards will mean using less concrete and steel and much more timber than previously so I guess it's all come full circle. I'd worked with Peter many years ago and although we didn't have a lot of official interaction on this project he was a common sight out on the ground. Peter is an original, that's for sure, and he not only has a sense of the big picture, but is constantly aware of the small details and can be just as attentive to them as the overall job. Our team quite enjoyed this project, as we were involved from start to finish. We went from digging holes and pouring tonnes of concrete to laying down those beautiful matai floors fifteen months later, so it was very rewarding for everyone. We like these big projects and this was a big job for Blenheim. And the fact that Peter was doing in fifteen months what others might develop over

several years took some getting used to. Overall it was a good project, good people to work with and we were very satisfied with the results.

The engineering project manager for Apollo was Peter Mann, who has since joined Yealands Estate as Sustainability Manager. It was his responsibility to oversee the mechanical innards of the winery, which, as noted, comprised almost half of the budget. Mann had just joined Apollo after stints with Fonterra and then Montana Wines, where he was the engineering manager, and he was immediately thrown in at the deep end with Yealands Estate. He had been involved in many big projects before this and was amazed at what Pete was doing at Seaview. Many of his previous large projects had been for Fonterra and he notes that when they took on big projects, the risk was spread among many shareholders. But here was just one man taking on the responsibility. As project manager, he remembers that Pete didn't make his presence felt too much during the workday – he'd let everyone get on with their work – but he'd see Yealands come out in the evening or on weekends and start wandering around the jobsite and you could guarantee that come Monday morning he would have a list of questions and suggestions.

The concept of sustainability was always a big part of the plan from the start. Every week for the first three months of construction, Peter Mann and building project manager Charmaine Boyd would get together for a design meeting with Peter. They would go over every aspect of the project with a special eye to keeping the sustainability concept in focus and also discuss new issues or ideas that had arisen. Apollo was not a stranger to this concept and between Paul Lloyd and Peter Yealands, a solid, comprehensive plan was put into operation. It was very important that any segments of the work that were specific to sustainability had to be implemented right from the start, as retrofitting could be very expensive and probably not as effective. Peter Mann recalls the concepts and implementation:

When confronted with the high levels of sustainability required, as an engineer I first saw it as more work. Everything, including all waste materials, needed to be measured and accounted for and I readily admit that my initial reaction was that it was going to be a pain in the ass. But the more we got into it, the more interesting it was. We discovered so many different ways that energy consumption could be reduced and it almost became a contest to see who could find the best ideas for energy reduction. This was not just for the build itself but just as importantly for the on-going production cycles that the winery was built to do. And as the work progressed we started to feel very good about it and what we were accomplishing.

The mechanical side is quite different than the construction of the build. With the building, you could see every day the progress you were making and could commission any extra work or people you needed as you saw fit. But with the mechanical parts, and this would include the refrigeration, the wine tanks, piping and so forth, you don't really know what's going to happen until that day when you turn the power switch on. And then even after that, much of the mechanical works don't get going until you actually have grapes coming in. That means that we had to very carefully plan all commissioning and set up a very rigorous timetable based only on our design work; trusting and hoping that all would go well when we turned it on.

I always enjoyed having Peter around the job site though. For starters he's extremely practical and was always coming up with helpful suggestions – along with many questions, I'll grant you – about the work that was going on. You have to remember that he had so much to do with the initial plans that to him the whole job was just the materialisation of things he had already seen in his mind. His knowledge is such that it was almost like a continual peer review of the work that was going on. And I never got the feeling that he was testing you, he was just curious about how the particular job was going to get done. It was a bit of a revelation for me as I had a lot of experience with other wine makers and while they always had a solid knowledge of how the actual winemaking machinery worked, no one had the overall practical engineering knowledge that Peter has. The irrigation system is a good example and when you see the size involved, you realise just how vast the irrigation system is. And of course it's mostly the work and design of Peter himself. To pull water up from the Awatere and then circulate it among 1000ha of vineyards was a staggering task in itself.

Advisory group member and winemaker Matt Thomson worked closely with Apollo in the production facilities and their interior requirements. The required volume of winemaking production had been pretty much determined and the building plan was based to a large extent on the size and number of wine tanks, which were all being housed indoors. The interior housing of tanks was an early prerequisite of the design. Outdoor tanks have some major drawbacks: outside is not always a friendly working environment, especially Seddon on a windy winter day; tanks sited outdoors have to be insulated and much of the equipment used, such as transfer pipes and cables, is UV-sensitive and would require regular replacement or special covering, again adding to the on-going expense. In the whole scheme of things, the cost of making the building large enough to house the tanks was actually comparable to the cost of outdoor insulation for the tanks. The interior location of the whole operation also results in much lower energy costs, adding to the reduction of the carbon footprint of the operation. The high level of the insulation afforded by sandwich panel construction of the building enables a corresponding high degree of energy efficiency and all required temperature changes can be carefully controlled. The extra bonuses are a much better look to the operation and a nice environment for people to work in.

There had been much thought put into the interior ventilation and heating and cooling requirements. Large exhaust fans turn on automatically when the CO_2 levels get too high and the building is set up to take advantage of interior/exterior temperature differences. Within the construction, the overall goal of sustainability actually proved to be a source of opportunity rather than problems for the building team. A significant fact of the construction project was that Peter did not tender any of the work. He and Paul Lloyd chose to work with companies, many local, who had comprehensive real-time knowledge of the industry and the land. Paul remembers that during the project, every previous assumption that everyone had was challenged and looked at carefully to determine how sustainability could be built into the project on a comprehensive and consistent basis. For instance, if a tank required moving to a particular location, the team would set a schedule that would allow two or more to be moved at the same time to reduce overall energy use.

Paul recollects the contribution of the various sub-contractors at the site: "Another advantage was that the companies who did the tanking, piping, electrical wiring and all the other jobs had far more expertise than any consultants – these were people who had to make things happen on a daily basis and had encountered any and all issues." There was complete cooperation within the contracting team to make the idea of sustainability work, and indeed Paul recalls that everyone saw the challenge as an opportunity. Many companies were involved, including Robinson Construction of Blenheim, John Jones Steel of Christchurch for the steel works, Active Refrigeration, Dawn Group for the pipework, Newpower Electrical, and Kingspan for the distinctive outer cladding of the building. Crown Tanks and Fulton Hogan were involved, along with many other smaller suppliers and contractors. Once Apollo had set the example of responsible recycling, the others soon followed suit and Paul recalls that there were really no issues or push-back from any of them.

Less than two years after that first meeting between Pete and Paul Lloyd over tea and biscuits in Vai's kitchen, the job was finished – on time and on budget. The big day had arrived for Peter Mann – his myriad tanks, pipes, connectors, conveyors and systems were going to be turned on and the process of making wine was to begin. He'll never forget it. "It was very hectic and busy and we were running around with all the usual work. It probably wasn't until that first truck was backing up with the first load of grapes that I felt a little nervous. Everyone was there, Peter, all the contractors and I remember thinking, 'I hope this all works'. The first thing that happens is the load is put onto the scales and weighed and shows on the readout and that worked so I thought, Well that's a good sign. And it was, the system did exactly what it was supposed to do and everything worked like a dream."

Peter Mann often refers to a simple model that clearly describes sustainability. It consists of three overlapping circles: one for society – the people involved and affected, one for economy – the business needs and profitability, and one for environment. In the middle, where the three circles overlap, is sustainability. This concept forces all planning to take all three aspects into consideration when implementing a viable sustainability plan. This model is used with all the staff so that they can see that it's not just a matter of "being green" and environmentally responsible – it includes the needs and duties of everyone involved.

The one very sad note was that shortly after the winery was completed, Peter's first sustainability manager, Harold Norden, died suddenly. The job title is not something you see in many industries yet, though with the emphasis on sustainability it will probably become more commonplace in the near future. That the job exists here is no surprise and Harold had been the perfect match for Peter. A former civil engineer and regional construction manager with Fulton Hogan in Blenheim, he had worked on various projects with Peter, including on the Kaiuma Estate subdivisions, before coming on board full-time at the winery. His primary focus with Yealands Estate was to manage and oversee the complete operation and attain the end goal of becoming and staying carbon-neutral. This requires an engineer's knowledge to monitor all the activities in the facility and work through all invoices and supply manifests to determine the extent of the enterprise's greenhouse gas emissions – including the details of airline flights, to accurately determine the total carbon footprint of the operation. He carefully measured all electricity and various fuel usages at the winery and once you've seen the extent of the production facilities, the scope and size of the work becomes apparent. Also considered, of course, is the cost and usage of fuels to transport the wine to their final markets here in New Zealand and all over the world.

A self-confessed perfectionist, Harold brought his engineering skills and a healthy passion for the environment to his role. He reiterated Peter's reasoning that as you get older you realise both the extent of environmental damage that has been done and the extent to which it can be prevented. Said Harold "When I first met Peter and started working with him, we had a meeting of the minds, as it were, and found we both shared a deep concern for the environment. I started doing some project management with him as he was having a bit of a time keeping a finger on all his various projects. When he asked for some advice in putting together a job description for a sustainability manager, I realised that I'd like to do it myself so in a way I've invented my own job. But that doesn't surprise me or anyone who works here – he's an inspiration to work with and the 'can do' attitude is refreshing and very rewarding." [15]

Harold's death was a huge blow to Peter and the whole Yealands team. Peter Radich recalls, "A major attribute of Peter has always been his ability to attract very good people to work with him. One of the key components to the Yealands Estate team was Harold Norden, now sadly gone, who brought systems and order to Peter's widespread business ventures and really enabled Peter to concentrate fully on what he excelled at, which was getting the actual job done. Harold was a real gentleman, with an outstanding mind, and it was a terrible tragedy when he died." Pete found an able replacement for Harold in the person of Peter Mann. Who better to oversee the operation than the man who built much of it.

With the job complete and wine being made, Apollo's Paul Lloyd could now assess just what they'd accomplished. He is happy to see that many things that were included in Yealands Estate Winery have now become industry standards. One example is that the usual temperature of the glycol used to cool wine tanks in Marlborough tended to be around -4^0C, but as it gets colder the energy efficiency decreases. They experimented and finally set the glycol temperature at 0^0C, which although it meant that the flow needed to be higher to achieve the same cooling effects, the overall energy costs were significantly lower. The tank jackets needed no extra insulation – another advantage of having the tanks indoors – and they found that they just needed a bit more time to achieve the required chill efficiency. Since this installation, several other wineries in Marlborough have recalculated their glycol temperature set-points as well. This was another result of the constant brain-storming sessions that were continually going on during the project to address the concept

15. Interview: Harold Norden with Tom Percy, August 2008.

of practical sustainability. Paul recalls that when the idea was discussed, nobody was really sure why the methodology behind the cooler temperature was the custom, including the winemaker, so they went ahead and the result speaks for itself.

The final piece of the energy puzzle will be the installation of large wind turbines. The area has been assessed by two separate power companies for the feasibility of wind power and both scored full marks for the potential of efficient wind-powered energy production. This will enable Yealands Estate Winery to achieve their goal of being energy neutral and to take it to the next step of producing power to go back into the grid. In fact one of the issues with this installation will be the ability and willingness of local power companies to take back power from the Estate when it is not being used by the winery.

Paul Lloyd has become a fan of Peter Yealands. He notes that there is no shortage of those who try to knock Peter for what he has accomplished and how he operates. Paul even went to the length of tracking down some insulting rumours that were floating around during the job. He took it upon himself to find the source and let them know that they'd been talking complete rubbish and blasted them for not fronting up to Peter himself with their nonsense. As he said earlier, he thinks of Peter as the perfect client.

> Peter had to trust Apollo – not easy when your own backside and a lot of money is on the line. We never had an issue that we couldn't resolve face-to-face in a timely and professional manner. And while Peter was around the site much of the time, there was no micro-managing or interfering. Not to say that he didn't mind mucking in himself from time to time – especially if it involved a bulldozer. Before the building actually began, Peter took the opportunity of getting out on his diggers and was responsible for the original landscaping and earthmoving that was needed prior to building. His personal involvement with the project was constant and while not telling others how to do their jobs, he kept a close eye on all aspects, especially expenses, of the project.

One telling tale involved the massive piece of matai that is the backdrop for the reception area. It is a big chunk of wood; very heavy and very oddly shaped. Peter had decided to use it after the builders had completed all the doors and entrance ways and the piece was too big for any of the doors. It was decided that the only way they could get it in was to lower it through the large skylight over the area, but the size, weight and awkwardness of the shape was making for a difficult job. At one point there were ten workers, a forklift and a crane involved but they still could not get it in. Finally, after a few hours of futility, Peter got fed up and sent everyone home. The next morning the crew showed up and there was the backdrop in place, properly mounted and anchored. Peter and son Aaron had somehow got the piece in with no discernible damage anywhere. Paul noted that the building crew's opinion of Peter's ability rose considerably after that. "In the end, the project displayed a total confidence from both sides. From Apollo's side we knew that we could sort out any issues quickly and pragmatically and from Peter's side he had complete confidence in our expertise and ability to get the job done to the mutual satisfaction of everyone."

Another upshot of the project is some keen rivalry to be and stay the most efficient winery in the country. Paul notes that a competitive winery in Hawke's Bay is making similar noises and so Apollo is continually monitoring the efficiency and energy input/output at Yealands Estate to ensure their leadership in the industry. Paul reiterates their original mission statement that the plan all along was to build and maintain the most efficient winery on a per litre basis not just in New Zealand, but in the world.

As to the project's overall economic impact on the area, Peter Radich had this to say:

> The property which Peter now owns would previously have been held by some eight families. Each of those families would have made a very modest income from those properties. It would be hard to imagine that any of those families would have had an annual net profit of more than or in some cases anything like $50,000. Each of those eight families in capital

terms, before we came on the scene, would have had an asset with a capital value in the range of $500,000 – $2,000,000. The gross earnings off these eight properties annually would in total have been less than $1,000,000.

Since Peter has taken over these eight properties the picture has changed completely. The overall capital value is in excess of $200,000,000. There would now [2008] be in excess of 100 people employed. The gross income from these properties is presently approaching $30,000,000 per annum and when the vineyards are in full production the gross income will be closer to $75,000,000. As well, these properties support innumerable service and other industries. Throughout the development, Peter was the largest client of a number of suppliers in Marlborough such as PGG Wrightson, Goldpine and the John Deere agency. In a small way I think that Peter can say that he has made a contribution to the New Zealand economy which has been worthwhile and which needs to be preserved and not put at risk.

In July 2008 the author interviewed Peter for the *Marlborough Express* upon completion of the winery, and this was the last question of the interview:

Q: So now it's done, the winery is running – is this the culmi-nation of your work, is this where it ends?
Oh no, absolutely not. We're an ambitious lot and we're looking at growing the business, adding more varieties right here and adding brands from elsewhere. Simply put, we want to be the biggest wine producer in the country. I've still got another 10 years of work to do, so you haven't heard the last of me.

Yealands Estate Winery officially opened on 8 August 2008. From the production of 5000 tonnes of grapes that first year, it is now working to its full capacity of 11,000 tonnes. The 2009 vintage produced 150,000 cases of wine and more than doubled that for 2010, with 350,000 cases sold. Peter has continued to innovate, and think many miles outside the square. He has introduced miniature Babydoll sheep to graze the vineyards without eating the vines. He has installed a huge burner/boiler system to burn prunings for energy to heat the water at the winery. He has sponsored awards and cash prizes for sustainability throughout the country. He has introduced plastic bottles. The wines are winning awards and the winery was honoured in 2010 by being named the most environmentally-pioneering winery in the world.

The Y-Team

Peter's insistence and ability to attract the best people is exemplified with his team at Yealands Estate. Gareth Goodsir, Vineyard Manager, Tamra Washington, Winemaker, and Michael Wentworth, Marketing Manager, head the team entrusted to grow the grapes, make the wine and sell the wine.

In the Vineyard

Vineyard Manager Gareth Goodsir is Marlborough born and bred and started working for Peter in 2005.

> I'd heard things about Peter but had never met him before he approached me about the job. The first time Peter brought me out here, there was just 65ha in production at that time but another 350ha ready to put into operation. It just seemed to me that here was something I could really get hold of. While I was over at Montana I'd seen what had been going on here the previous eighteen months, and to be honest I thought, "What's this silly bugger doing, trying to put grapes in over all those hills." But I did a bit of homework before I took the job and figured it would be quite a job. We're up to 1000ha now, so I've seen a lot of change around here in four years.
>
> I've always enjoyed working outdoors and being a practical, hands-on kind of person. And if you're in Marlborough and like working outdoors, the wine industry is the place to be. As far as the sustainability side goes, to be honest when I was a young guy I couldn't really give a toss. Put it down to youth

I guess. But being around Peter, that's obviously changed and now I find it a very important and challenging part of the work. Everything we do out there is channelled towards sustainability and it really keeps you focused on the general concepts and the actual application of the concepts all the time. And it's not just PR – it has become the way we do things and the results speak for themselves in so many different ways.

At the busiest time of the year we have 170 people on the ground, twenty-five of which are on permanent payroll. Most of the offshore workers we have are from Thailand and they're an absolute dream to work with. We have to actually stop them working at times; they're very family oriented and are sending money home to support their people. To be honest they put a lot of younger Kiwis to shame the way they work. I cannot think of one single incident of trouble we've had over four years. They're just great. We house them on site in many of the old original farmhouses and we've built new units as well. They're equivalent to a good back-packers' hostel and it's an easy decision for us to take good care of them.

I've now worked with Peter for four years, and three and a half of those we worked together on a daily basis. You certainly have to be the right kind of person to work with him as he expects others to work as hard as he does – and he works hard. But he's very fair and takes good care of those who work for him. And what he believes becomes the way everyone does their job and the end result is that though it's taken a while, we're all fully on board with sustainability. We've had the odd row, though thinking about it perhaps no more than five or six times over four years. And I'll think, "Why am I putting up with this crap" but after blowing a bit and going off and thinking about it, you get over it. And of course the worst part is that nine times out of ten, he's right. The best way to get your own ideas implemented is to suggest it a few times until finally Peter will come up one day and say, "You know this might work better if we try it this way." But he's a treat to work with. In all the time

I've been here I've never once heard him raise his voice and he's always calm. He never puts anyone down and is extremely honest and when the bloke you work for consistently behaves that way, you find that everyone else tends to behave the same way so it's good for everyone. He's also a good teacher and will always take the time, so it's easy to come to work every day.

One of Peter's innovations was the use of animals to graze the vineyards to keep fuel costs down and keep the use of herbicides to a minimum.

Mowing the grass at a 1000ha vineyard uses a fair bit of fuel so we're looking to these miniature sheep to help out. Since the winery opened, we've experimented with a range of alternatives to traditional tractor mowing. It began with regular sheep but unfortunately they developed a taste for the grapes. Our second idea was to use guinea pigs although this proved unviable on a commercial scale, though they will be missed by the hundreds of harriers, falcons and hawks that dined regularly on the poor wee buggers. I had to put up with some laughable media attention with that idea and I guess it's one time when I probably deserved it.

His latest idea is one Peter is convinced will have major environmental benefits: because Babydolls only reach 60cm tall when fully grown, they are no threat to the grapes. The newest arrivals are being grazed amongst 125ha of Sauvignon Blanc vines that will be grown organically and are attracting interest from local and international winegrowers. They were imported from Australia and didn't come cheap at close to $3000 a head. They had to spend a few months in quarantine as well but they eventually arrived, much to the delight of the last surviving guinea pigs. Peter plans to cross-breed the Babydolls with Saxon merino and grow the mob to 10,000. This will provide additional opportunities in the textile industry and there's also a possibility to sell niche cuts of meat to restaurants. The sheep can often be seen on one's way into the winery. They're cute little things although Peter says that while they're trying to speed things up, the sheep insist on breeding at their own pace.

Making the Wine

Winemaker Tamra Washington is regarded as one of the rising stars of New Zealand's wine industry. Only in her early 30s, she's already captured attention for crafting award-winning wines in Europe and now returns to her hometown to head the Yealands winemaking team.

It's the ultimate prize, working with super premium cool-climate fruit and facing the unique challenge of being involved from scratch in the set-up of a new winery and wine brand where there's a total commitment to sustainable principles. It's been such an interesting experience. I've been here from the start so to be here when all the systems went in and to have had such a major role in the installation has been very exciting and challenging. It's taken a while to get to know the variations in the vineyard, understanding the quality and the styles coming up in the vineyard and working with them and putting the team together.

Tamra finds that compared to previous positions she's held, the system is much more efficient, though she admits that it was quite daunting to start from notes on paper and work to a finished bottle of wine. The system is very sophisticated, using the latest technology and software, and she wasn't sure if and how it was all going to work out. But the start-up was virtually trouble free and within a few weeks she was able to fully concentrate on the job at hand – making good wine.

Tamra knew little about Peter when she took on the job. Growing up in Marlborough she'd heard the name and knew that he had "hands in lots of pies" but wasn't aware of his latest endeavours. Although Peter had no experience making wine, Tamra knew that he had a lot of experience setting up vineyards, and she'd known lots of hands-on owners in Europe who thought they knew a lot about winemaking, but who usually only knew enough to be the nuisance you couldn't tell to go away. If anything, Tamra saw Peter's inexperience in winemaking as a plus and Peter was very straight-up about his lack of knowledge, telling her up front that was why he was hiring her.

One of the major aspects of the job was the whole concept of
sustainability. I wasn't really aware of it when I first applied
but as I looked further it became apparent that sustainability
was going to be a cornerstone of the business, which I thought
was pretty cool. I knew that it wasn't going to compromise
the winemaking at all, in fact I was pretty sure that with the
systems in place to monitor every bit of energy going in and
out, if anything it would make my job easier. And so it's been.
I'd seen some shockingly inefficient wineries in Europe and was
looking forward to the set-up here. He's really got it right as far
as I'm concerned and I know I've never seen anything like it in
the world.

Tamra has been left to do her job but knows that Peter is never
far away. But his disinclination to micro-manage coupled with his natural curiosity has made for a very enjoyable working relationship between
them. Even though Peter's office is up front and Tamra's lab is at the back
of the complex, she finds that when she has to go the front of the building
for some reason, she and Peter will end up chatting for fifteen or twenty
minutes.

And has the dedication to sustainability changed Tamra's ideas of
making wine?

Yes it definitely has. In Europe I saw some pretty shabby
behaviour as far as energy and waste goes. It had really shocked
me at the time but I gradually got used to it as it was just part
of my day-to-day. I went back once and was again shocked,
especially with the mindset and application that we have here.
It has made me very much aware of what we're doing and what
we're using to make things happen, obviously from the energy
side of things, but also other things as well. As far as the actual
winemaking, it's had absolutely no negative impact whatsoever. I'm free to make the wine, use all of my experience and
knowledge and get on with it. It's just that the added concept
of sustainability has made me more aware of what we're using

from an energy standpoint. The monitoring is all worked into our system so it's no biggie and anyway I think it's pretty cool what we're doing and how we're behaving.

The biggest learning part of Tamra's work here has been getting to know the grapes and what they and she are capable of producing. The vineyards are not one long flat section of exactly the same grapes, but of varied terrain. Some of the more exposed areas produce distinctly different grapes than vines in more protected areas. The vineyard also runs lengthwise up from the sea, stretching several kilometers, which also becomes a factor in the flavours and nuances in the grapes. There is still a lot of work to do in the vineyard that should be very beneficial. In the section that is being grazed by the Babydoll sheep, the vines will be trimmed to just two canes. This will increase the quality per vine and Tamra will be experimenting with selected blocks to see how the different yield will affect the grapes. She has found that overall the fruit is very good from the vineyard, showing intense and varied flavours through all varieties.

There are some inherent challenges working in a very large vineyard with variations in terrain. One major issue is mitigated by the fact the winery is in the middle of the vineyard, so transport and monitoring of the grapes is not an issue. However, the biggest challenge is the variations themselves. Peter made every effort when setting it up to ensure that each block was distinctive and uniform, but there is still some spill-over associated with the terrain. Ripening is not always uniform so harvesting requires careful attention and timing to get it right. Tamra wants everything to be as consistent as possible and this has been an area that she pays considerable attention to. She works very closely with vineyard manager Gareth Goodsir, especially during vintage, and they monitor each block on a day-to-day basis. They will carefully plan what is to be picked and when and Tamra will get the inside staff properly prepared while Gareth prepares his team. It has been and continues to be a (forgive me) fruitful relationship and has been crucial to overcoming the main challenge of producing a consistent product from such a large area.

The upside of the size of the area, however, is the potential it provides to accommodate the inherent variety into Tamra's winemaking and this has already shown itself in the broad spectrum of flavours that she has to work with. Everything is kept separate and Tamra can often access up to seventy different Sauvignon Blancs all with a slightly different shade of flavour. To a master winemaker like Tamra, it offers an exciting choice of blends to work from and has already manifested itself in the many awards that Yealands Estate wines have won. It is also a moveable feast, as each vintage brings a new mix of flavours to work with, resulting in variation from year to year. It also allows Tamra to pick and choose as each year passes and select those that were exceptionally good to maintain the quality of the wine through each vintage.

Tamra admits that for a new company the volume of production is considerable, but with the systems that were put in place from the start, the volume has not impacted in a negative way. The winery owns all its equipment for harvesting, Gareth has his team in place, so getting everything harvested in time is achievable, and they are never dependent on outside issues that could compromise the harvest. The facilities are such that if need be the whole vineyard could be harvested in ten days. The production itself was geared for this tonnage from the beginning and poses no issues for Tamra's side of the operation. It is again testament to the meticulous and comprehensive planning that went into the facility and the willingness of Peter to ensure that nothing is spared in keeping the operation doing what it was planned to do.

Tamra also agrees with Peter that people should be able to purchase a good bottle of wine for under $20. She knows that the winery's goal is to produce fresh, interesting wines that exhibit good flavour and represent good value. She knows that her skills combined with the equipment and technology at hand should ensure a consistency of quality across the brand spectrum. They have neither the desire nor the expectations of marketing wines selling for $60 or $70 a bottle. That was never the plan and as Tamra says she would hate for people not to be able to afford a bottle of their wine. She is fully confident that Yealands Estate wines can and will hold their own with any New Zealand brand and that their marketing is dependent not on the opinions of "wine experts" but on the tastes and buying habits of regular folk. Tamra is quite firm on this:

This is a quality product. We maintain the highest levels of quality throughout the process, all the grapes are from our vineyard, we know what we're working with and can pretty much control everything to keep within our standards. The price of a bottle of wine is not always a determining factor of its quality. I saw wines that I made in Italy being sold in the UK for £4–5 a bottle, and I knew better than anyone that it was good wine. I like making good-value wines and I want as many people as possible to enjoy them.

In the end, Tamra's goal is simple – she just wants to make good wine. And she knows that this is only possible if the material she gets from the vineyard is of the highest quality and can be accessed fully and at the right time. So far both of these prerequisites have proven to be spot on and she still sees a lot more potential as time moves on. For Tamra, it is a complete cycle – from the vineyard, to her, to the wine in the bottle on the shelf. She is fully in step with Peter: his concept of sustainability, his plans and aspirations for the winery and Tamra again proves Peter's belief that the best investment you can make is having the best people to do the job. "Peter loves being involved. He gets excited about all sorts of things big and little. He especially likes to help out with what may seem a trivial issue or something small that will help make things work better. He's just a great guy and a wonderful boss and I love working for him."

Moving the Juice
Marketing Manager Michael Wentworth's job description is basically three words – sell the wine. Says Michael:

With the amount of wine coming on board, we have to find a home for it all. It's important that we protect the brand, and we're also developing private labels. The first six months we found it very difficult to get any momentum going, but then quite suddenly, and coincident with the European summer, things just started to take off. When all the contacts we'd been working on finally moved, they moved big and we haven't really looked back. I've also been quite surprised at the complexity of being involved in every aspect of marketing and not just a specific channel or product. We've added many new labels and they all need marketing in their own specific way. Here you're expected, and have to be aware of all areas of the distribution, sales, marketing, etc. It's provided me with a much broader knowledge of the business and it's been quite a big learning curve, but absolutely no regrets.

In November 2009 Michael and Peter made one of their regular trips to Europe and the UK.

Peter is very focused on backing up the product and the story with our marketing and distribution skills. The story is unique – Peter is a real person with a great story – green, carbon zero, sustainability, people had even heard of the guinea pig experiment. A good example is one of the major wine shows in the UK – basically a warehouse full of wine and lots of men in suits – and there's Peter. He's a bit of a magnet and people just want to come and talk to him. The story is great, the distribution network is growing rapidly, and is all backed up by the product. He loves telling stories and people just hang off every word when he does, but when someone pays him a compliment he just brushes it off and usually deflects it to someone else.

Once we get product into people's hands, that's 90 per cent of the battle – it's a good product and lends even more credence to the whole story of Yealands Estate. Good marketing will get the wine into people's hands the first time – then the wine itself brings them back again. And distribution backs this all up so that the product is available. Peter gives you a free hand to get on with the job but he likes to know what's going on. Due to the rapid growth and expansion of the marketing efforts, I do feel that he gets a bit frustrated at times with not knowing everything that's going on. But every morning, Pete and I sit down for half an hour or so and get a catch-up on everything.

2010 has been a great year and we expect to do over 350,000 cases, which is pretty much everything we can make ourselves. We're actually a bit worried that we may not have enough wine in the tanks to fulfil all our orders, so while that's a bit of a nuisance I suppose it's not a bad problem to have. We do like to keep our consistency for our customers so we'll have to see how that works out. We feel we're on a definite roll now – it took a while, especially as we really started from scratch, but we've got a really good momentum going. The overseas distribution is going very well as we're now in over thirty countries. We've expanded our sales and marketing team and are continually growing as new markets and new opportunities emerge.

In mid 2010, Yealands Estate signed an important distribution agreement with Les Grands Chais (GCF) of France. The GCF Group, founded in 1979 by Joseph Helfrich, has become the leading French wine and spirits trader, with a turnover in 2008 of over €700 million, more than 70 per cent of which was from export. With the exceptions of Africa and South America, GCF distributes everywhere in the world. The connection between GCF and Yealands Estate was suggested by one of Peter's banking people in Europe and after making contact and presenting their story, Yealands signed on and will be reaping the benefits of this world-class distributor for a lot of new, mostly European business. GCF has some significant similarities with Yealands Estate in that both are operated by one person and both are very much aware of the need and value of good marketing. Michael feels that some good synergy is already apparent in the relationship and notes that Joseph Helfrich and Peter Yealands are cut from similar cloth. Indeed GCF had made it clear to Yealands that they really prefer to work with family businesses and it has already proven to be a good fit. The two-way agreement gives Yealands a lot of freedom to seek markets on its own and the agreement has no bearing on distribution relationships that Yealands has already established. Michael notes that this is yet another example of the many "right time, right place" relationships that Peter continually gets involved in and wonders if perhaps some other-worldly serendipity is an inherent part of the Yealands mystique.

Another very significant agreement was reached in 2010 with Pão de Açúcar, a massive retailing entity in Brazil. They are the biggest Brazilian company engaged in business retailing of food, general merchandise, and other products from its supermarkets and other stores. The company has over 1800 stores throughout Brazil and is also the biggest retail company in Latin America by revenue. As there are very few New Zealand wines currently being distributed into Brazil, Michael sees this as a huge opportunity for Kiwi wines in general and Yealands Estate wines in particular. In 2010 other international outlets were established in Denmark, Sweden, Czech Republic, Hong Kong, Fiji and new opportunities in Russia, Japan, Thailand, Singapore and Chile are being developed.

Previously established and flourishing markets still include the UK, Holland, Germany, Canada and the US. The UK market has been especially positive for Yealands Estate. Their relationships with Tesco, Marks & Spencer and Sainsbury's are the mainstay of their UK business, most of which is handled through their UK distributor, Liberty Wines. Michael accompanies Peter on many of these overseas trips and has seen how Peter has become more attuned to the business's needs and is that much more enthusiastic as each new market becomes apparent. For an erstwhile stay-at-home, Peter has become an enthusiastic marketer, travelling the world to help establish the brand.

Michael has also seen the reality of sustainability in their marketing efforts and feels it is a great way to get your story told and becomes a good way to get your foot in the door. Once that door has been opened, it's invariably quality and price that keeps it open and maintains the revenue stream. Tesco in the UK was a good example as they are very much dedicated to sustainability and the Yealands story was a natural fit for their corporate viewpoint. Sustainability is currently a much bigger issue in Europe than in America and the Yealands approach has served them well in that market. Michael notes that many of their European contacts are regularly asking about the stories that revolve around Peter. Whether it's the Babydolls or the plastic bottles, everyone seems to know some aspect of the Yealands sustainability saga.

On the domestic front, two major initiatives were launched in 2010. The most newsworthy and notable was the introduction of plastic bottling for some of the Sauvignon Blanc under the Full Circle label. Michael notes that while the environmentally friendly aspect was the initial impetus for the label, it's the practical side of the product that's really surprised him. First reaction to Full Circle has cited the convenience of the product and has proven to be a big hit with trampers, boaties, festival attendees, indeed anywhere where weight or glass restrictions prevail. People heading to the summer bach and off-site caterers have also been very positive about the product, which is smaller and only 10 per cent of the weight of a standard glass bottle. Michael acknowledges that the plastic bottle has been a polarising issue – while being roundly flayed in the media by wine purists, it was also being touted as interesting and convenient from those with a more practical bent. Purists were stuck into the "plasticky" taste and "denigration of the New Zealand brand", but all of this was laid to rest when the Full Circle Sauvignon Blanc won a silver medal at the Royal Easter Wine Show in 2010. The label is produced in small runs to ensure freshness and in 2011 a non-estate merlot will be added to the Full Circle label.

Plastic Bottles?

As one may imagine, Peter has a fair bit to say about the plastic bottles. The plastic bottle venture is, in his words, "going good, going remarkably good". The Full Circle label is limited to a very small percentage of Yealands' total output and at time of writing is only being marketed for domestic consumption. Nonetheless, Peter does not see this as an experiment, stating that he would never launch an experimental product.

The usual negative comments, especially from wine buffs who are still not over screwcaps and bemoan commoditization without really understanding or wanting to understand what the move was about. This along with lazy research in some of the early media stories, implying that Yealands was replacing glass altogether with plastic, didn't help. There were wine critics who sniffed and moaned about the "plastic under-taste" but few were inclined to blind taste-test it alongside wine from a glass bottle.

Whatever the case, Peter couldn't give a toss about what these critics think. It's not only a solid marketing move but fits in with his concept of sustainability. The Full Circle plastic bottles are 89 per cent lighter, generate 54 per cent less greenhouse gas emissions and use 19 per cent less energy to produce than traditional 750ml glass bottles. And while Sauvignon Blanc was the only varietal to carry the Full Circle label originally, a merlot was added in 2011.

Setting up the bottling infrastructure was the most difficult aspect of the product launch – their regular bottler did not have the resources and the plastic used is not the usual soft-drink-bottle plastic; it has a specific oxygen-scavenging component. But the lower bottling and recycling costs and weight advantages, coupled with the quality of the wine inside are the only relevant factors. And Yealands is not the first in the world to make the change – Wolf Blass in Australia is bottling in plastic and British supermarkets Tesco and Sainsbury's are marketing wine in plastic bottles.

It's not for everyone, but younger generations will get into it. There are wine buffs and then there are people who buy wine in supermarkets. More than 70 per cent of Sauvignon wine is sold in supermarkets for under $20 and is drunk within a week. That's the market. It's also being used in the little bottles you find in hotel mini-bars, it's been selected for airline use and we are also very proud to see that the wine has been selected for shipment to Antarctica. We've had some very nice compliments from trampers, for the obvious reasons, so overall we are very happy with the response.

Yealands Estate bottled its first run of 5000 bottles of Full Circle in 2009 and the bottles carry an 18-month use-by date, even though the bottle manufacturer assures 1000 days before any deterioration is noticeable. The move has been described as "brave" by Master of Wine Bob Campbell, but others are not so sure. Full Circle plastic wine bottles look different to regular bottles – smaller in height and width and significantly lighter. A traditional wine bottle weighs 500gms whereas a Full Circle bottle weighs only 51 grams. The lighter bottle also means significant emission reductions and cost savings for exports. A traditional pallet of wine carries 56 cases of wine but with Full Circle packaging can fit up to 72 cases, and the cartons themselves are made from 100 per cent recycled materials.

From the start we wanted Full Circle to be the most sustainable wine in the New Zealand market. Our winery and wines are already carboNZero certified, but this takes sustainable wine production to new levels. It'll never be for everyone but it's not made for everyone, so I don't really know what all the fuss was about. And the wine has already won a silver award at the 2010 Royal Easter Wine Show – and what was notable there was the judges didn't know the wine was from a plastic bottle.

Also in 2010 Yealands took over their own distribution within New Zealand. They had no issues with Hancocks, who had been handling their domestic distribution, but this had been a long-time goal of Yealands Estate. Being in charge of their own destiny and having direct relationships with their customers were the two big factors in their decision. Peter feels that their current volume of domestic sales is below where it could be and this is a step in increasing them. Michael reiterates Peter's feeling that it's always nice to do well at home. They will still be selling through wholesalers and their current New Zealand sales team will take on more responsibility in their quest to increase New Zealand sales.

Michael is glad he made the move from the corporate world in Auckland.

There has been not one day that I've ever regretted making the move down here. It is continually refreshing and a completely different outlook moving from the corporate life. And working with Peter is very special. He's a guy with extremely strong morals and this is reflected in all his dealings with everyone – staff and customers alike. His focus has shifted somewhat in there being less time on the tractor and more time in the office. He's also a very quick learner and has absorbed so much about the industry, especially the marketing side of the business, since I've been here. The market has been tough over 2009 and 2010 and I think that there are only two or three wineries, us included, that are making headway in the current economic climate. We've kept growing and Pete has stuck to his guns on his yearly planning schedule, to the point that we're actually a year ahead of where we planned to be when we started out. And I think to do that in a down market really says a lot about everyone here.

We've been fortunate in that Pete is not afraid to invest and bring on board some very good people. And we're masters of own destiny somewhat in that we always know how much wine is coming down the pipeline and have been able to plan effectively and in a timely manner. We've got such a good management team here and everyone has always bought in to what Peter wants to accomplish. Looking down the road we're committed to getting up to a million cases a year by 2013. We have the capacity right here at Seaview to produce that volume so I see it mainly as Marketing's responsibility to make that happen. We want to be one of the top five wineries in New Zealand and one of the top five New Zealand wine exporters globally as well, so we've got lots on our plate to keep us busy. I know that Pete is always looking for ways to grow faster so we may just get there a little sooner but get there we will.

Mission Accomplished

What started over tea and biscuits has come – to steal a label – Full Circle. Of the many awards, articles and accomplishments that Yealands Estate has engendered, perhaps the one that is most indicative of Peter's vision is the 2010 award from the Great Wine Capitals Global Network. The Great Wine Capitals is a network of nine major global cities, in both the northern and southern hemispheres, which share a key economic and cultural asset: their internationally renowned wine regions. It is the only such network to encompass the so-called "Old" and "New" worlds of wine, and exists to encourage travel, education and business exchange between the internationally renowned centres of Bilbao/Rioja, Bordeaux, Cape Town, Christchurch, Firenze, Mainz/Rheinhessen, Mendoza, Porto and San Francisco/Napa Valley. In November 2010, Yealands Estate was judged "The most environmentally pioneering winery in the world" and was the only New Zealand winery to win an international award from the

Network. In December 2010 Peter looked back at what has been accomplished and what the future holds for the winery.

It's an interesting phase at the moment what with the strife in the industry. Fortunately, because basically we're performing so well and against the trend I suppose, we're probably the only reasonably sized winery that's growing to the extent that we are. In 2010 we added three million litres of capacity and spent somewhere in the $5 million range in expansion. We're recruiting staff and we're selling wine like it's going out of fashion. But I think we've got another year or so of tough times before the surplus if you like – though I don't really believe that it's a surplus, I just think it's under-marketing – is sorted out.

What I have learned here is that distribution is key – it's the make or break of this business. We've recently made the step of taking on our own distribution for the New Zealand market and that will be interesting to see how that works out. Internationally over 50 per cent of our sales are direct to the buyer, and we also have distributors in America, the UK and in Australia. And for the direct-to-buyer market we do a lot of private labels outside of what the distributors handle. With our private labels we're generally free to go wherever we like. We've recently added distributors in Brazil and several in Asia so outside of New Zealand we're going great guns.

I think the industry still has some hard times ahead of it but we're not standing still. I've got a good team and good bank support and we are going to grow this business so that we can be up there with the handful at the top. As we go forward we'll be looking at growth outside our own boundaries, such as organic growth, and we'll be looking at buying vineyards or wineries. That's the plan and it's all based on economy of scale – I feel you need a million cases a year to get there. We will get there – the vineyard has the capacity to do a million cases a year but I just love challenges ahead of me, and I don't just want to sit back and wait until this vineyard gets fully mature in 2013. We launched out here in August 08 into a bit of a headwind and I believe that when the wind changes, we're really going to fly. We've got a massive vineyard and a lovely winery so I'm very optimistic. We're in a good space.

As to the future, I expect to be pretty involved in this for the next five years or so. But this has grown to be quite a big company and right now it's just Vai and me. We're both getting close to our pension time if you like, so another five years may just about do it. I really have no other interests except working here and to me it's not like work. I haven't had a holiday for ages and everybody is saying, "Why don't you take a break?" but I've got no real interest in going on holiday. All I want is right here.

CHAPTER ELEVEN

A Bloke For All Seasons

Think boldly, tread lightly and never say it can't be done.

How does one take the measure of a man? Some are judged by what they say, most would like to be judged by what they do, but as often as not it is the opinions of others that give an unflinching indication of a man's true character. Words are often quickly forgotten and deeds over time get taken for granted. It is one's interactions with people that leave an indelible imprint and tell so much of who that person really is.

Over the years, Peter has interacted with a lot of people and if there is one constant it's that very few people forget Peter Yealands. You hear all the "larger than life" and "force of nature" stuff, but every now and then someone comes along and fits those clichés and Peter is one of those people. Superlatives soon get worn out in trying to describe what he has accomplished so it is hoped that the preceding account of his life and career speaks for itself.

All that he has done pales in his own mind to the importance of his family and his friends. His daughter Danielle notes that he is by nature "a quiet and simple man". He doesn't see his accomplishments the way others do. If somebody points out to Peter that he has accomplished things that very few other people have, he gets a little defensive and says he doesn't see it that way at all. He even challenges you to come up with things that he's done that others haven't and it's not false modesty – he just seems to think that he's carried on in his usual way. If it's pointed out to him that perhaps he started out doing what others do but has taken it so much further than others he just shrugs and reckons everyone's entitled to their own opinion.

I like to think I've been a good citizen for the community and I sleep easy at night with very little on my conscience. I've never done a bad thing that I can recall or certainly never deliberately done anything bad, so I'm not a malicious sort of bastard. I guess invariably over your life you cross swords with the odd person but I prefer not to. It's very easy to lose a friend and usually harder to make one. I think I've been a little bit fortunate to get into a few things at the right time.

As regards to what I've done over the years, I confess I don't really think too much about it, although obviously some do. Sometimes I'll wait outside the airport rather than going in until just before boarding, especially on local flights. If I go in it seems I get bombarded with questions and comments. I don't like being in the limelight and I never have. I've been in it over the last few years and I know I have to do everything I can to drive the sale and promote the company. When I'm asked to talk anywhere I get nervous as shit, but when you get a good crowd and get a good reaction then it's not so bad. I suppose I'm getting a little better at public speaking but it's not really my strong suit. I thought perhaps about learning how to do it a bit better but then I don't really want to be different to what I am – can't make a silk purse out of a pig's ear can you.

What you get with me is what you see. I'd really prefer to be in the back seat and I've always been like that. By the same token, I enjoy good company and love getting into a good conversation when the time and the mood is right. So I'm not antisocial but I'm certainly not overly social and don't really go looking for it.

Another constant is the opinion of those who know him and work for him and that they are disarmingly candid in their respect and admiration of him. Over time he has occasionally rubbed a few people up the wrong way but as previously noted, the reputation for butting heads has become somewhat inflated over the years – though it makes for a good story. The reputation, the snowy beard, the long hair and work clothes – sometimes he's just too easy a target to ignore.

That reputation played front and centre in the media during the Oyster Bay takeover battle and not always in a positive light. But then you have to remember that most of those media folk work in the big centres where Peter isn't, and they'd prefer to keep on the good side of the perceived powers that be. Peter was constantly portrayed as a nuisance, a gadfly, a thorn in the side – it made for good copy. But few took the time or made the effort to find out what really drove him and were quite happy to let him play the country bumpkin role. Even many in Marlborough think that Pete is a "love him or hate him" kind of bloke.

Good Friends

Bruce Hearn is a long-time friend and an early pioneer of mussel farming. "What drives Peter? He just wants to conquer things – to be first, to create and he never does things by half measures."

> The new vineyard and winery are prime examples of his mindset, though I don't think he does it for public recognition – he does it for his own self-satisfaction that he figured out the situation and got it sorted. And this whole sustainability thing is something he has a real passion for – it's not just for appearances or trendiness or anything like that, he's dead serious about it. It's never been about money – he just wants to be out there.
>
> The whole family is quite remarkable – I'd often say that they'd get a good idea at ten at night and by next morning they'd have it built. It might not always work on the first go, but they'd stick to it till it came right. And Keith was fifty when they started into mussels and neither he, nor any of the boys for that matter, ever shied away from the work – and believe me the mussels were hard work back then.
>
> Peter went down to Kaiuma and almost disappeared for ten years or so. When he started showing up on the rich list, we were really surprised – we had no idea but of course he had property all over the place. But we thought that he'd probably

stay down there for the rest of his life raising his family there. As it turns out I guess ten years down there let him play with his diggers and bulldozers and recharge his batteries and start to look for the next big thing.

Peter Radich recalls when he first met Peter in the early 1970s. Pete had started his hay-baling business and was a client of the legal firm that Radich had recently joined:

> One of my first jobs there was collecting unpaid debts from some of his customers. Whether they were slow to pay or whether Peter just never got around to doing it himself I don't know. But there I was going after $50 here and $100 there that was owed to him. We also ended up being nearby neighbours for quite a while on what was then Fell Street in Blenheim. Peter and I were nearly the same age and both were starting our young families.
>
> Peter is a person totally devoid of nasty behaviour or maliciousness. He is very even-tempered, remarkably calm under pressure and very stable in a storm. This has translated into him exuding such quiet confidence that it rubs off on those around him and those who work with him. He is very clever and intelligent, keeping in mind that of course he hadn't had much schooling to speak of and virtually no specialised training of any sort. I've noticed that he also has a remarkable capacity to absorb and process information – much more than anyone I've ever known. He can analyse this information accurately, take to heart the bits that are valuable and discard the rest and so get on with the job. Peter has a vision that others just don't have and this uncanny ability to look at something and see what it can be, and to know what has to get done tomorrow morning to make it start happening.

Jim Jenkins has known Peter since the very early mussel days and believes there are several things that drive Peter:

First of all, it must be the genes because his dad was just a superb businessman. I think that there is also a supreme confidence perhaps bordering on arrogance that allows Pete to get on with these big jobs and projects without being held back by fear, including fear of failing. I saw the odd time or so when an idea of his didn't quite work out and he just figured out what the problem was, sorted it, and went back at it. It just doesn't worry him. He was always just a little ahead of most others and could smell a deal from way off.

And he's never changed – here's one of the richest men in the country and I'll occasionally run into him in the local supermarket pushing a cart around looking for bargains. I've known Peter for a long time and to be honest, I'm a little surprised that he hasn't sold out of the wine industry yet – he was always looking for the next big thing, but perhaps he wants to see this one out. I think he's won the media battle in the Oyster Bay thing and has proven, to me anyway, that he's right and that he's the better man. As regards to the mussels, Peter has to be considered a major driving force to the early success of the industry. What he did, and did first, especially with regards to the infrastructure and supplies, made a huge contribution. I have never seen or heard of Peter being dishonest and to me he is the ultimate entrepreneur. Peter is that maximum Kiwi bloke.

Murray Mears is probably Pete's oldest friend and certainly for many years they were inseparable. They worked the mussels, put companies together, got into some mischief and did a lot of hunting and enjoying each other's company. Murray still manages Pete's three vineyards in Blenheim and though they don't see each other as much as they used to, it is apparent when speaking with either one of them that the bond is still there.

He's been a good mate – he's always done right by me and we've worked together for thirty years or so. We had our share of rows but it was never anything that wasn't forgotten by the next day. Mostly it was Peter wanting to work a few more hours, or do one more load – always squeezing that last little bit out. I think it was the second or third year out at the Grovetown vineyard and things were going well and Pete said if we got a good harvest he'd give me a bonus of 1 per cent of the crop. And that year everything around town got frosted but we didn't and we had a massive crop. He hadn't set a price and ended up getting somewhere around $4,000 a tonne plus harvesting and the vineyard cleared a million dollars. And he kept his word and I got a ten-grand bonus.

When Pete had the row with his family, it bothered him a lot. I always felt, and I think he did too, that his dad and brothers sort of ganged up on him but then I only saw it from Pete's side. I think that was another thing that spurred him on though because when he got something new on the go and got busy, it didn't seem to bother him as much. Things smoothed over in the end but there were always niggles with the boys. But then most families have their rough spots, and being in business together didn't help either.

Always a family man

For Peter it has always been about his family. As a young boy he was pretty much left on his own after the twins were born and he became accustomed to getting on with things by himself. It was not that he was shunned by Keith and Dorrie, but it seemed they knew that Pete could look after himself and they, with good reason, were very concerned about the twins when they were young. After Pete and Vai were married and Aaron and Danielle came along, Pete had what perhaps he had missed for many years. Aaron has worked with Peter virtually all his working life; Danielle is now back living in close proximity – and Peter couldn't be happier.

If anyone knows Peter, it's Vai. Vai is not just Pete's wife; she's his partner and, obviously, has been a major influence on his life and made it possible for him to do what he does.

Peter's never been one to have to rely on others to make things happen and with the winery he knew that it just didn't make sense to depend on the spot market or trying to get contracts to sell the grapes. And Peter's never been one for half-measures. He's always planning; in fact I can remember that when we lived at Grovetown, he used to draw plans on the toilet wall. And where most of us would look out on a paddock and see a paddock, he could always see what it could become.

I guess I've got used to his always jumping into new projects over the years and while it may seem a bit haphazard to many he always does his homework and gets good people around him. Of course now with the winery and all, he's had to get out in front of people a lot more and that's very difficult for him. He's basically a shy and private person and used to be very shy with people he didn't know, but he knows it has to get done so he gets on with it.

Asked when he realised his dad was not quite like other men, Aaron said he figured it out when he was about five years old. As soon as he started going to school, he saw that other kids' dads left for work at eight and got home at five, but not Peter. He'd be gone by seven and not home till late but was there most Sundays. It just became normal to Aaron and didn't really bother him. He gets on well with his sister, Danielle, and they spent a lot of time together as kids. He was ten or so when he realised that Peter always worked for himself and didn't work for other people.

I remember when I was still at school and I was helping Dad paint the bridges up the Awatere River. My payment for helping set up the sand blaster and keeping all the paint mixed was I was allowed to sit on the bonnet of the old Corona car with a shotgun, driving up and down the Awatere valley with a box of shells shooting at rabbits and pigeons to keep them from crapping all over the fresh paint. Once the box of shells was gone, that was it – that was my pay. I think we have a good relationship – both work-wise and as father and son. And I think he appreciates the effort I put into everything. I always do the best I can at every job that comes along.

Dad seems to have a pretty good knack at leaving a landmark behind. Not sure what drives him – he just likes to do bloody well at anything he does do. I remember once at North Bank after clearing a large paddock that was covered in gorse and worse, Dad said, "That's the last time I go through this nonsense," but of course that attitude only lasted until the next opportunity came along.

From spending all his working life with his father, Aaron caught on quickly that Peter demands very high standards and has adapted the same for himself. Aaron comments on the loyalty that Peter engenders. "Generally the ones who can't or won't do the job properly are the ones who get sacked anyway and the good ones tend to stay around. When people have had to be let go just through attrition or lack of work, most don't want to go and look to get back again, and many do."

Working with Peter, Aaron concedes that he and his dad have had their ups and downs but they blow over quickly and Aaron really likes working for his dad. "He's a good bloke to work for. If you want something, like a hoist for the shop, you ask, make a good case and justify the need and he'll say go out and get it. Dad has helped out with workers' families if a serious need comes up, but doesn't make much noise about it – just takes care of his people is all. And Dad usually gives preference to someone who needs a job over someone who just wants a job."

What Peter has accomplished strikes Aaron most when he's been into town or somewhere else and is returning home. He comes over the hill and literally everything he can see is Yealands Estate and he knows that not many men can or have done this. "What he's done here is bloody spectacular."

To daughter Danielle, "Dad was always a man who does things, but it hasn't been until the last few years or so that I've realised that he's different from other men."

He was always trying new things and developing new things

but lately the projects have been on a very large scale. He was always interested in seeing things change or making things change, and always for a practical reason, not just for the sake of tinkering.

Aaron is three years older than me and we were always pretty close and are good friends. He started working for Dad when he was 14 and I would be down at the workshop after school. For me, it was a comfortable place to be and all the people there that I knew well. A nice thing about Mum and Dad is they very rarely had rows or anything like that. Mum was and is a very tolerant and supportive woman and I'm sure that Dad wouldn't have been able to do many of the things he did if he hadn't been with her. She has her limits, but she always seems to know when to go along and when not to.

At some point, I'd really like to see him, perhaps not stop, but at least slow down. I really think he's missed a lot with what some may call an addiction to work, but of course to him he's just getting on with the next step or next thing on his agenda – which is always full! We've had this argument, though he'd say discussion, and he always says he's happy with what he's doing and it's what keeps him going. But I have seen a change in his later years – he seems to have a bit more interest in cultural things and is more socially comfortable. When I was younger, unless he was with his mates, he was actually quite shy in social situations. He's always enjoyed cooking though he doesn't get into the kitchen that often. And it's a little ironic him owning this big winery because I can remember that when he occasionally drank wine, it would be out of a fruit juice glass. But he's coming along.

There is part of me that would like to have had more of Dad, more of the man – he was always busy and quite hard to reach at times. Like any child I always wanted to impress my dad with what I was doing and I'd be looking for some sort of approval from him. He's very limited with his accolades so when you do get them you know that it's special. But you know that no matter how busy or unreachable he may be at the moment, if you ever need him he'll be there. I hope he takes the time to get away from all this from time to time. Get him on a fishing boat with no phones or anything – I think it would do him a world of good. I'm very proud of him and very proud to be a Yealands.

The last word

We're a long time dead and quickly forgotten and I think you're much better off having a go and failing than to never have a go at all. I think it's all summed up in our trademark banner. Think boldly, tread lightly, and never say it can't be done. And it's not for the money.

Money was just never that important to me. As long as I had enough to do the next project I was happy. And in spite of all this recession and whatnot, my mindset will never change. I'm still full of ideas and enthusiasm and the idea is when I sell something off, I'll find something to replace it. I've got lots of other ideas, though whether I'll get them done I don't know. The way I look at it, the day I run out of ideas, I might as well die.

I think the world's in a mess at the moment [late 2010]. There's no doubt about it. You've got all the productivity and currency issues in the EU. Whether it's going to lead us into a double-dip recession I don't know. There's all the money printing in the States, third world countries that want to keep their values low so they can keep selling their products to the developed world, the developed world with really no desire for their products. I suspect we'll get by but the currency situation is a bloody mess. When you see a 20 per cent difference between the Kiwi and the American dollar in a fortnight, how can you plan for that? The fluctuations are that great that there's no way you can accurately hedge. I know most people think that there's bugger-all you can do but if everyone took that view we'd be totally stuffed. I try and do my bit and I'm still very bullish about what we're doing here. We've learnt the hard way recently that nothing's forever and that what goes up comes down, but by the same token what goes down comes up. It's all a matter of timing and us priming ourselves for when it does.

One of the lessons I've learnt is never be afraid of borrowing money, because you'll never do anything big without borrowing. Borrow it wisely of course and do your homework. Another thing is for anyone to be successful you have to learn to be able to delegate. That's the key and if you can't delegate you'll be very limited as to what you can do yourself. And another thing that was hammered into me by my father is never hesitate to employ people better than yourself. You'll find that if you bring really good people on board, they will be a magnet for other good people. Most of the people that work for me now in senior management are far far brainier than I'll ever be. I think my skill, if you could call it that, is that of mid-dle-man, a catalyst, an instigator or whatever you want to call it.

The rich list? First thing I can tell you is that I never ever wanted to get on the list. They call and you tell them to bugger off, but they go and do their own homework and seem to think they know what they're talking about. The rich list I believe has little to do with how much money people have in their pockets. It's based more upon their assets versus their loan exposure. So when they said I had assets of $70m, I probably had closer to double that, but unless I'm mistaken and I hope I'm not, they can't know the specifics of your bank debt. I've always said they are wrong – and I don't say whether they're wrong up or down – and that it's my own business. There was one year when I was the only person in Marlborough on the rich list so I suspect that there are other people out there that are far wealthier than me.

The other thing is that I don't value wealth by way of money – money is a f***ing evil thing. It's nice to get by on and all the rest but it causes more strife than it's friggin worth. I don't like losing money but I don't have any high aspirations of living. Since 2007 I've been drawing a salary here – it wasn't my idea but my accountants kind of held a gun to my head on that. For the previous 25 years I'd just live off the business – take what I needed when I needed it sort of thing. So here I am drawing this salary now – it goes straight into *my bank account and it's just sitting there. I might take a few dollars from time to time but I'll bet 95 per cent of what I've drawn is still sitting there. We live on the smell of an oily rag. You can see that, with the house and all. I don't like these flash cars – all you end up doing is worry about them getting dinged. I love my old Blazer, though Vai is telling me it doesn't really fit into the green image so I suppose I'll have to change at some point.*

Then there's the rumours. All of my tractors have been repossessed – actual fact is I sold a very big tractor that I'd had for two years and wasn't using it anymore. I had the option of getting the money, but just took it off a hire-purchase agreement. I own twenty John Deere's, two of which are on hire-purchase, I own the rest. Next rumour is Rabobank is foreclosing on me and I'm selling out to an Australian company – complete rubbish. Next rumour is my wife has left me – that started when Danielle was very close to her second baby being born so Vai took her over to Nelson for the birth.

You know it's very hard to cover your ass and your face at the same time. For instance I publicly went out and said I was looking for an equity partner for the winery – still looking but not very hard with the current climate. I've probably been the biggest individual spender in Marlborough for the last four or five years – I've literally spent millions. But the thing is that with all these capital assets in these economic times, because nobody is buying, these things really have no value. And when there's no market, people tend to look hard at you, and you look hard at yourself too. And I've looked hard at myself and said that this is going to be extremely tough – this is the worst recession I can recall.

The only way to get through it is to sell off your non-core assets and rethink what you're doing without trying to stir up too many pots. But it's very hard when no one is really buying. What do seem to grow well in this climate are rumours. I have to sell a tractor – must be in trouble. Looking for an equity partner – I must be in trouble. Kaiuma is also being affected. Because there's absolutely no interest whatsoever, I've put the whole scheme on hold and that just starts another rumour mill.

To finish up on the rumours, what I can say is I have full support from my bank and we owe nothing to creditors. So it's all a load of crap and you can try to refute it but that just seems to make it worse so in the end I just ignore and let it die out on its own.

So yeah, I'm at peace. I'm rapt now that I've got my family around me, especially the grandchildren. Vai and I still have reasonable health, though I'm getting a bit lazy – too much sitting behind this bloody desk. I'll jump on the old grader on the weekend and it knocks the shit out of me now. I don't really have too many other interests. I like to watch the All Blacks and used to watch a bit of cricket but don't really have the time now. I've been getting out boating a bit with Aaron and keeping an eye while he's diving and that's good. Aaron and I have always worked together and it's good having him and his family here. And now Danielle is just down the road with her kids and it's just great. Danielle and Vai are very close so it's been good for both of them and I'm getting to know her kids better.

I might be a hard bastard to get close to – I don't know. I don't have many friends out there – it seems the only time I get a phone call on the weekends is because somebody wants something. And that's probably a bit sad but I guess it's my own doing, or lack of my own doing. I get invited to join all sorts of bloody things but I tend not to. I'm fine right here, that's the way I am, and Peter's Peter.

Peter certainly is Peter; a plain man with simple values who accomplishes complex and marvellous things. While not a "greenie" *per se*, he embodies what perhaps greenies should think about more often. He has taken his beliefs and commitment to sustainability and molded them into practical, professional and profitable enterprises that benefit the community, provide hundreds of jobs and celebrate the best of what New Zealand is to the rest of the world. He is a man of his word, yet says few. What he has done says a lot and how people feel about him says even more. Peter Yealands is indeed a bloke for all seasons.

APPENDIX

All stories and headlines from the *Marlborough Express*.

27 February 1974

SOUNDS MUSSEL INDUSTRY HAS COME TO A DEAD STOP

The development of the mussel farming industry in the Marlborough
Sounds has come to a dead stop. Government departments have been
delaying the issue of leases to those involved in the projects, in one case
for four years.

The "strongest possible terms" will be used in a letter from the Marlborough Harbour Board to the Minister of Agriculture and Fisheries,
Mr. Moyle, the Board decided yesterday. Some of the large mussel growing rafts are already in use in the Sounds, but last year the Marlborough
Harbour Board decided not to allow more such craft until Government
leases were granted...

Small rafts used to catch mussel larvae or "spat" are not so heavily embroiled in red tape. There are many of them scattered about the
Sounds, but their loads of spat are building up and their owners cannot
transfer them to the bigger growing rafts.

One of the mussel farming concerns is the N.Z. Marine Culture
Company. A principal, Mr. P. Yealands told Captain Jamieson that his
firm had 3,500 long ropes laden with young mussels and no more licensed
rafts to attach them to.

"We have six spat rafts in the Keneperu Sound and each one is absolutely loaded with ropes, due to the fact that we cannot have bigger spat
rafts or more than two in good catching areas," Mr. Yealands said in a
letter to yesterday's meeting. "We are busy building rafts as it will take

about 25 rafts to farm the spatted ropes we have now, provided the spat stays on them. We realise that we have aggravated our problem to some extent by being enthusiastic about this new industry, but then we did not know that a licence can take up to four years to be processed."

Because of the policy set last year, Mr Yealands will be told that a request for approval to put in growing rafts is declined.

11 May 1974 – MUSSELS AND SCALLOPS GROW WELL IN THE SOUNDS.

29 May 1974 – MUSSEL FARMERS MAY RECEIVE GO-AHEAD FROM HARBOUR BOARD

3 June 1974
SOUNDS BOARD'S MOVES OVER MUSSEL FARMING.
Some farming businesses have been held up for long periods, one since 1969. The Harbour Board has become increasingly upset over the delays in the issue of the necessary leases and permits, delays which apparently stem from the Ministry of Agriculture and Fisheries. If there is no action by late this month, the Harbour Board will make its own moves and will allow mussel farmers to site their rafts in approved situations. It will not be a blanket approval and each application will be examined on its merits.

26 June 1974
BOARD GIVES GO-AHEAD TO SOUNDS SHELLFISH FARMERS.
The N.Z Marine Culture Company will be allowed to place its rafts in Mills Bay, Keneperu Sound. The Board approved the move yesterday, and the rafts will be licensed as moorings.

27 August 1975
MARINE FARMING TO BE "OFFICIAL" SOON.
Some years after the first application was lodged, the Ministry of Agriculture and Fisheries is about to issue the first marine farming licence for the Marlborough Sounds. Marine farmers in the still experimental industry

have been working for some time under temporary permits issued by the Marlborough Harbour Board.

One of the industry's pioneers, the N.Z Marine Culture Company will have the first licence which will cover operations in part of Ruakaka Bay, Queen Charlotte Sound.

September 24, 1975 – MUSSEL FARMS AND LAWS ALARM BOARD.

Alarmed by the current flood of applications for marine farm sites in the Sounds, the Marlborough Harbour Board has decided to stop allowing more mussel farmers in while Government offices consider applications.

4 October 1975 – MORE CONCERN OVER MUSSEL FARMING.

30 November 1975 – MARINE FARMING LICENCE FOR SOUNDS FINALLY GRANTED

5 January 1976
BUREAUCRACY FRUSTRATING LOCAL MUSSEL FARM FIRM

"Unless this officer does what he promises, we stand to lose our 1977 mussel harvest," an angry and frustrated Mr Peter Yealands said today.

Mr Yealands, with his father and two brothers run N.Z. Marine Culture Co., the biggest local mussel farming enterprise with 20 rafts in Pelorus and Queen Charlotte Sounds. The officer he referred to is with the management division of the Ministry of Agriculture and Fisheries and in charge of issuing marine farming licences.

Two years ago he assured the Yealands that they would have their licence for Mills Bay by Christmas. Last year he said it was only a week away. Before this Christmas he said it was on the way and that he would advise the Marlborough Harbour Board that the licence would be signed so that the board could allow spat rafts to be positioned.

The board received no advice so on Monday Mr Peter Yealands telephoned the officer again and received another assurance that a letter would be written to the board and a phone call made. Neither was carried out, it is alleged.

The officer was contacted again, said he had posted the letter but could not telephone because the telephone was out of order. By this morning neither letter nor telephone call had been received by the board. The only hold-up with the licence is that it still has to be signed by the Minister.

The Yealands are anxious to get on with it. They are catching spat but are losing it as fast to fish feeding on it. They want to protect their spat catch by placing a net around the raft to keep the fish off but are not allowed to since the harbour board, in conjunction with other local authorities decided not to allow any more activity in marine farming unless licences had been issued.

The board decided on this step once applications for mussel rafts flooded in without MAF issuing licences. The board sought to force the ministry's hand and has. The first licence was issued late last year to N.Z. Marine Culture Company for its four rafts in Ruakaka Bay.

Mr Peter Yealands said that they had no gripe with the board. They could understand their concern and even though this stop-go business affected them detrimentally they could understand the reasoning behind it.

"For four years we have been trying to make a go of this new industry. We have sunk a lot of capital into it and a lot of man-hours. We are at the end of our tether and about broke, but we continue because we know the industry has a great potential."

He thought it ironical that one government department encouraged the new industry through tax incentives while another hampered it through procrastination. The family had sunk more than $50,000 in the venture and more than double that if labour was counted he said.

Mr Yealands said they understood the concern of the harbour board and other local authorities about not permitting rafts without a licence. Ever since Mr Jim Jenkins of the Fisheries Industry Board had returned from Japan and reported on the possibility of using ling lines rather than rafts, applications for marine farming licences had come in thick and fast.

"There's a lot of speculation in these applications. Licences can be transferred and people want to get licences so that they can sell them later.

All sorts of people apply – doctors, lawyers, clerks. They are from all over the country and some call on us to pick our brains. When we tell them our story, they don't believe us because they think we want to put them off. Some of the applicants know nothing about mussels, some don't even know there are two types.

"We have co-operated all along with the authorities. We even built a raft free of charge for the Fisheries Industry Boards for its experiments, and supplied it with gear. The board has helped us in return. We are now the biggest marine farming company in the South Island and have just received export orders to Noumea. It won't be long before we are a big industry if we are allowed to get on with it. We can sell all we can produce.

He said the company had come far, despite the setback of nature and bureaucracy but if a licence was not granted this week, as promised, it could prove to be the straw that broke the camel's back.

30 April 1976
MUSSEL FARMERS GET LICENCES AT LAST
Marine farming licences have been registered for Mr Bruce Hearn and N.Z. Marine Culture Ltd. (the Yealands family).

The Member for Marlborough, Mr Edward Latter today announced that the two licences had finally been signed, sealed and registered. "The licences have at last come through and I compliment T*he Express* for highlighting the slowness of the bureaucratic system processing the applications." Mr Latter said. "I am pleased for the Yealands and Mr Bruce Hearn who can now get on with developing their new industry."

Mr Peter Yealands was relieved at the news. "We can now go ahead and put more rafts in. We will be assembling a raft at Havelock tomorrow and add it to our rafts at Mills Bay. We got a terrific catch of spat and the potential for our 1977 harvest is between $80,000 and $100,000.

Mr Yealands said that export prospects were excellent. Their marketing expert Mr. W. Walker of Porirua had just returned from Australia with an order for three or four tons of mussels in the shell per week. And therein lies some trouble. The demand for mussels in the shell is good, the market for mussel meat is small.

"I saw a new condition on our licence. We are not allowed to export mussels in the shell. I don't know why that is. Australia wants them frozen in the shell and is not interested in shucked mussels. The shells are clean and uniform and allow a better presentation of the mussel. I don't want to say much about that condition. I am too pleased about finally getting the licence but we will have to take that up with the department later."

Mr Yealands expressed his appreciation of the work Mr Latter had done to get some finality with the licences. "He has done more than we expected and more than anyone else ever did in Wellington for us."

22 May 1976
MARINE FARMERS TO WAIT A LITTLE LONGER
Prospective marine farmers will have to wait a little longer. That was the general message from yesterday's meeting in Picton of all parties interested in the industry. The meeting was called by the Marlborough Harbour Board and all local authorities and Governmental departments involved.

The Board chairman Mr H.J. Stace said the meeting was called because of frustrations and exasperations in the administration of marine farming licences. The Board was unhappy about it and wanted to take over the administration job to speed it up.

PROBLEMS LISTED
Mr Paul Currie of the Ministry of Agriculture and Fisheries listed the problems to be sorted out before an application became a licence. These were numerous and ranged from water purity, cadastral precision of the sea surface, from seaworthiness to indemnity.

Mr Currie said he had received 69 applications for mussel farming. He expected 18 licences to be offered to the applicants by the end of June. If they could comply with the conditions, mainly for exact survey, their licences would be issued. The 18 were for the applicants who had spatlines out. The procedure for a licence had two stages, he said – a statutory period of four months to allow objections, followed by seven to eight months at least "for technical and administrative reasons".

Mr Currie said it was "essential" that the area be precisely surveyed.

This could take months and could cost the applicant $600 to $700. An environmental impact report could be required and this could take two years.

Mr Rowling wanted to know why it still took six weeks to offer licences to the 18 applicants who had spatlines and stood to lose them. Mr Currie said the minister had not yet decided on the objections.

Mr Rowling also wanted to know why it should take two years to decide on an environmental impact report. That, said Mr Currie, was a matter of policy which he could not explain to the meeting but would give to Mr Rowling in private if he wished.

BIBLIOGRAPHY

Berry, Ken, *Scrutiny on the County*, Marlborough County Council, 1986

Dawber, Carol, *Lines in the Water*, River Press, 2004

O'Carroll, Brendan, *Barce Raid*, Ngaio Press, 2005

O'Carroll, Brendan, *Kiwi Scorpions*, Token Publishing, 2000

INDEX